BASEBALL LEGENDS
of All Time

Publications International, Ltd.

Contents

Introduction

The history of baseball lies in the history of its players—from Ty Cobb's relentless pursuit of excellence, to Babe Ruth's zestful pursuit of, well, just about everything. Throughout baseball's colorful history there have been players with considerable statistical totals, and there have been those whose leadership and strength of character gave them the ability to win

TY COBB HELD ALL MAJOR BATTING AND BASERUNNING RECORDS IN BASEBALL AT THE TIME OF HIS RETIREMENT.

ballgames. Above all of these, however, some players were blessed with both attributes. These are the players whose lives have become synonymous with the game—the all-time greats, the immortals. In *Baseball Legends of All Time*, 116 of these all-time greats spring to life in over 250 dramatic pictures and insightful biographies.

Names such as Aaron, Gehrig, Mantle, and Mathewson inspire images of awesome brilliance on the baseball diamond with sensational, late-inning home runs, unbelievable catches, and unhittable pitches. To

CHRISTY MATHEWSON'S THREE WORLD SERIES SHUTOUTS ARE A MAJOR-LEAGUE RECORD.

achieve the status of legend, a player must make these kinds of plays on a regular basis, and the players included in this book did just that. Consider Mickey Mantle, whose 18 home runs and 40 RBI in World Series play are the most ever, or Lou Gehrig, with an unparalleled 2,130 consecutive games played and a lifetime batting average of .340, or Hank Aaron and his 755 home runs, or Christy Mathewson's 373 victories on the mound—these feats are not merely record-book accomplishments, but are testaments to the tenacity and enthusiasm which a gifted player brings to the game.

LOU GEHRIG AND BABE RUTH COMBINED FOR HUNDREDS OF YANKEE RUNS. A MORE FABLED DUO IN BASEBALL HISTORY MAY NEVER SURFACE.

OSCAR CHARLESTON SLUGGED HIS WAY TO COMPARISONS WITH BABE RUTH.

In addition to players from the National and American Leagues, you will find several legendary performers from the Negro Leagues. Throughout the 1920s, 30s, and early 40's, the Negro Leagues flourished, providing all the excitement and intrigue of the other major leagues, and giving rise to many remarkable careers. American and National League clubs would regularly schedule exhibition games with Negro League teams, and even Cuban League clubs. Oscar Charleston of the Indianapolis ABCs managed to hit 11 home runs during these exhibitions. In a 1910 12-game exhibition series in Cuba pitting slugger Pop Lloyd's Chicago Leland Giants, an independent Negro League squad, against the Detroit Tigers, Lloyd went 11-for-22. While the Tigers won seven games, Ty Cobb (who batted .370) was sufficiently embarrassed (having been easily thrown out on several stolen-base attempts) to vow never again to play against blacks. In fact, Lloyd's 1911 New York Lincoln Giants team drummed Connie Mack's powerful Phillies club 9-2, beating Hall-of-Famer Grover Alexander in the process. As a testament to the competitive level of the Negro Leagues, Joe DiMaggio once said of Satchel Paige, "[he] was the best I ever faced."

A legend can, quite simply, do things on the baseball diamond that other players cannot. Were it no mean feat to win the Triple Crown, Carl Yastrzemski would not be the last man

JOLTIN' JOE DiMAGGIO HIT SAFELY IN 56 CONSECUTIVE GAMES, A RECORD THAT STILL STANDS AND IS SELDOM CHALLENGED.

to do so since 1967, and Bob Gibson would not be the last NL pitcher to win both the MVP and Cy Young Awards for his 22-9, 1.12 ERA 1968 season. These accomplishments serve to indicate the enduring nature of the game of baseball, and the historical longevity of those who played the game the way it had never been played before.

The pages of *Baseball Legends of All Time* bring offensive greats such as Ted Williams and Harmon Killebrew to the plate while pitching legends including Lefty Grove and Walter Johnson take the mound.

TED WILLIAMS TWICE CAPTURED THE COVETED TRIPLE CROWN.

Step into the Yankee dynasty of the '50s with Joe DiMaggio and Yogi Berra, or pull for their cross-town rivals, the Brooklyn Dodgers, with stars Jackie Robinson and Duke Snider. *Baseball Legends of All Time* includes all the names that have made baseball our national pastime for generations.

MICKEY MANTLE SUCCEEDED JOE DiMAGGIO AS THE NEXT YANKEE STAR.

Hank Aaron

On April 23, 1954, Hank Aaron hit his first of 755 major-league home runs, a higher total than any other player in big-league history.

Henry Louis Aaron (born 1934) grew up in Mobile, Alabama, learning baseball by hitting bottle caps with a broomstick. By 1951, he had signed with the Indianapolis Clowns of the Negro Leagues.

The Milwaukee Braves signed Aaron in 1952. The next year, he helped integrate the Sally League, and led the circuit with a .362 batting average and 125 RBI.

Called up in 1954, Aaron's impact was almost immediate. He paced the NL with a .328 average in 1956 and won MVP honors in 1957 with a .328 average, 44 home runs, and 132 RBI. Milwaukee took the World Series that year as Henry hit three homers.

After succeeding most of his career in a terrible hitting environment, Aaron and the Braves shifted to Fulton County Stadium in 1966, a great hitters' park. In 1970, he became the first to collect 500 homers and 3,000 hits.

On April 8, 1974, Aaron shattered Babe Ruth's record of 714 homers. Racism and reverence for the Babe made the task even more difficult, but

Henry's determination allowed him to achieve his goals.

He batted .300 14 times and hit 30 or more homers in 15 seasons. He drove in 100 runs 13 straight years and ended his career with

AARON'S SMOOTH STROKE LED THE BRAVES' ATTACK FOR 21 SEASONS.

2,297 RBI and 6,856 total bases, both major league records. Henry entered the Hall of Fame in 1982 as perhaps the greatest righthanded hitter ever.

Grover Alexander

In 1911, Grover Cleveland "Pete" Alexander won 28 games, a modern rookie record, and set National League rookie marks for strikeouts and shutouts (since broken) on the way to a 373-victory career.

Alexander (1887-1950) won 29 games in the New York State League in 1910, and was purchased by the Phillies. In 1915, his 31 wins led Philadelphia to its first pennant. The following season Alexander scored 33 victories, including an all-time record 16 shutouts. He won 30 again in 1917, becoming the last to total 30 victories two straight seasons, let alone three.

The Phillies then traded Pete to the Cubs, who lost him to World War I early in 1918. Serving on the front lines in France, Alexander lost hearing in one ear after a shelling and also experienced the first

ALEXANDER HOLDS THE MODERN RECORD FOR COMPLETE GAMES (436).

symptoms of epilepsy. Between shell shock and the illness, Alexander relied more and more on alcohol for solace.

After returning from overseas, Pete rejoined the Cubs and had several more outstanding years. Waived to the Cardinals in early 1926, "Old Pete" had enough left to win nine games in the Cardinals' successful pennant drive.

In the 1926 World Series, Pete started and won both the second and sixth games. In game seven, when the Yankees loaded the bases with two out in the seventh inning, Alexander was called on to protect a 3-2 Cardinals lead. (Legend says he was hung over, but his teammates swore he was sober.) He fanned rookie slugger Tony Lazzeri, then shut down New York over the final two innings.

His improbable and storied career ended in 1930, and he was named to the Hall of Fame in 1938.

Cap Anson

Adrian Constantine Anson (1852-1922) was perhaps the most influential on-field figure of baseball's early years. Not only was he a top player, but an innovative and fiery manager as well.

After signing in 1871 with Rockford in the National Association, he joined the Philadelphia Athletics and remained with them through 1875. The next year, Anson and several teammates jumped to the Chicago White Stockings of the new National League.

A wizard with a bat, Cap batted under .300 only three times in his 27-year career, registering a lifetime .329 mark, and collected exactly 3,000 hits—becoming the first to do so. Cap also led the National

League in RBI nine times between 1880 and 1891. Furthermore, he paced the loop twice in batting average and three times in slugging percentage. As a player-manager, "Pop" led Chicago to five pennants. He also was the first to institute spring training for players.

Anson was not without flaws, however. His vile on-field language often drew fines from umpires, and he was called "Crybaby" due to his endless complaining. Moreover, Anson believed the major leagues should be the province only of white players. Because of his efforts, blacks were barred ("unofficially," of course) from big-league playing fields until 1947.

During the 1897 season, Anson lost control of his players, and White Stockings president James Hart demanded that Cap resign as manager. Anson

ANSON ONCE EJECTED THE WHITE STOCKINGS OWNER FROM A GAME FOR SUGGESTING A PLAY.

refused, and was fired. After leaving baseball, Anson operated several businesses and starred with his family in a vaudeville act. In 1939, Anson became one of the first five men to be elected to baseball's Hall of Fame.

Luis Aparicio

Shortstop Luis Aparicio, who patrolled American League infields from 1956 to 1973, was one of the best fielders ever at the position. He teamed with Nellie Fox to form one of the top keystone combinations in baseball history.

Luis Ernesto Aparicio y Montiel was born in 1934 in Maracaibo, Venezuela. His father, Luis Aparicio Sr., was the best shortstop in Venezuela for 25 years. Junior took his father's position on the town team in 1953, and was signed by Chicago the next season.

Luis debuted with a splash, winning the 1956 Rookie of the Year Award by hitting .266 with a league-best 21 stolen bases.

The "Go-Go Sox" finally won the AL flag in 1959, finishing last in home runs but first in steals. All-Stars Aparicio and second baseman Nellie Fox led the league at their positions in putouts, assists, and fielding percentage. Fox won the Most Valuable Player Award, and Aparicio was second in the voting. Luis also led the Baltimore Orioles to the 1966 world championship.

His 56 steals in 1959 led the league, and represented a new level of performance for Luis. He posted totals of 51, 53, 31, 40, and 57 from 1960 to 1964, and only one rival swiped over 30 bases in that span. He won nine consecutive stolen base titles, something no one else has done. Along with Maury Wills and Lou

FLEET-FOOTED APARICIO WAS A SEVEN-TIME ALL-STAR.

Brock, Aparicio ushered in the running game of the 1960s.

Aparicio's glovework sealed his 1984 Hall of Fame election. He was an unparalleled defensive player. Luis played more games at shortstop (2,581), was involved in more double plays (1,553), and registered more assists than any other shortstop. He won nine Gold Gloves and led his league in fielding average eight times and assists seven times.

Luke Appling

Luke Appling never reached the World Series, didn't play flashy defense, and hit only 45 career homers, but he sustained a remarkable level of performance for many years. Appling batted over .300 sixteen times in a

APPLING'S .388 IN 1936 IS AN AL RECORD FOR SHORTSTOPS.

20-year career, and collected 2,749 career hits.

Lucius Benjamin Appling (1909-1991) was purchased in 1930 by the White Sox, for whom he would play his entire career.

He became the full-time shortstop in 1933 and won the first of his two batting titles in 1936 with a career-best .388 average. He was named the outstanding major-league shortstop by *The Sporting News*, an honor he also received in 1940 and 1943. Appling also drew nearly 90 walks a season, leading to a career on-base percentage of .396. He once fouled off 19 pitches in a single at-bat.

Luke hit .317 in 1937, but a broken leg in 1938 robbed him of some speed and range. In 1940, he lost the batting crown to Joe DiMaggio, .352 to .348. Appling won another title in 1943 with a .328 average, but then went to war, missing the entire 1944 season and most of of 1945.

Pushing 40, Appling hit over .300 each year from 1946 to 1949. He always seemed to have an injury, and his constant moaning led to the nickname "Old Aches and Pains." When his average slipped to just .234 in 1950, he retired after 2,422 games.

Luke set big-league records for shortstops (since broken by Luis Aparicio) in games and double plays, as well as AL marks for putouts, assists, and total chances. Appling, voted into Cooperstown in 1964, remained in baseball as a scout, coach, and manager for many years, and homered in the first Crackerjack Old Timers Game, held in 1985.

Richie Ashburn

Richie Ashburn was one of the best defensive center fielders ever and a consistent leadoff hitter who led the NL in on-base average four times.

Ashburn had only 29 career homers, but he was a potent offensive weapon. His career on-base average was .397, and he scored over 90 runs nine times.

Signed by the Phillies' organization in 1945, Don Richard Ashburn (born 1927) overtook defending NL batting champ Harry Walker for the starting center field slot in 1948. Ashburn hit an impressive .333 that season and paced the NL with 32 stolen bases. He also fielded a league-best 3.1 chances per game.

Ashburn and the Phillies won the NL pennant in 1950 as Ashburn hit .303 and again paced National League center fielders in putouts and total chances. On the last day of the season, the "The Whiz Kids" won the pennant from the heavily favored Brooklyn Dodgers. Ashburn saved the game in dramatic fashion for the Phillies when he threw out Brooklyn's Cal Abrams at the plate in the ninth.

THE DURABLE ASHBURN WON ROOKIE OF THE YEAR HONORS IN 1948.

"Whitey" Ashburn manned center field in Philadelphia through the 1950s, compiling a streak of 730 consecutive games. He won two batting crowns— in 1955 hitting .338, and in 1958 with a .350 mark.

Ashburn hit just .264 in 1959, and the last-place Phils traded him to the Cubs. For Chicago, he hit .291 and paced the NL in walks for the fourth time. Before the 1962 season, he was sold to the expansion New York Mets, who went 40-120. Ashburn, voted the team's MVP, hit .306. ("'Most Valuable Player' on the worst team ever? How exactly did they mean that?" he asked later.) Ashburn retired after the season with a .308 lifetime average, and became a Phillies broadcaster.

Frank Baker

Despite only 96 career home runs, "Home Run" Baker was a great offensive player, leading the AL in round-trippers four consecutive times and RBIs twice. He was easily the best third baseman of his time.

John Franklin Baker (1886-1963) joined Reading of the Tri-State League in 1908 and was purchased by Connie Mack for the Philadelphia Athletics that summer.

In his rookie season, 1909, Baker hit .305 with 19 triples (still an American League yearling record). Two years later Baker received his "Home Run" nickname when he topped the AL in four-baggers and clubbed two more homers in the World Series that fall against the Giants.

Between 1912 and 1914, Baker teamed with first baseman Stuffy McInnis, second baseman Eddie Collins, and shortstop Jack Barry to form the "$100,000

BAKER HIT **93** HOMERS—AN AWESOME TOTAL CONSIDERING THE LONG BALL WAS NOT A LARGE PART OF THE GAME.

infield." The 1912 season was Baker's best, as he led the AL in homers and RBI and hit .347, a record for junior circuit third basemen

that stood until George Brett batted .390 in 1980.

After the A's were embarrassingly swept in the 1914 World Series by the "Miracle" Braves, Mack broke up his team by either trading high-salaried stars or refusing to pay them what they were worth. Baker sat out the 1915 campaign when Mack tried to cut his pay. The following year, the Yankees purchased Baker from the A's, but a year away from the game apparently affected him as he hit just .269.

When his first wife died in 1920, Baker again retired temporarily. He returned to the Yankees the following spring as a part-time player, but retired for good, in 1922, with a .307 career average. The Hall of Fame summoned Baker in 1955.

Ernie Banks

Ernie Banks's reputation as a fan favorite and goodwill ambassador should not obscure his ability. He was a fine fielding shortstop, a great power hitter, and the first National Leaguer to win back-to-back MVP Awards.

Born in 1931, Ernest Banks was signed by the Kansas City Monarchs, one of the top Negro League teams. He played one season there before serving two years in the Army. After his 1953 discharge, Ernie returned to the Monarchs. Major-league teams were interested in Banks, but Monarchs owner Tom Baird

would only sell Ernie's rights if Banks skipped the minors. The Cubs agreed, and made Ernie their first African-American player.

Chicago's everyday shortstop in 1954, Banks hit .275 with 19 home runs. The next year, he batted .295 and clubbed 44 taters, including five grand slams. Banks hit .285 with 43 homers in 1957, and the following season was the first MVP winner from a sub-.500 team when he led the National League with 47 home runs (the most ever by a shortstop) and 129 RBI. In 1959, he won the award again by slugging 45 homers and again pacing the league in RBI. He also led the NL with 41 round-trippers in 1960.

"MR. CUB" HIT AN NL-RECORD FIVE GRAND SLAMS IN 1955.

Banks was a fine shortstop for nine seasons, winning a Gold Glove in 1960. A nine-time All-Star, "Mr. Cub" moved to first base in 1962 as a result of knee injuries.

Banks hit his 500th home run in 1970, appropriately at Wrigley Field, where he spent his entire 19-year career. He remained a hero in Chicago after his retirement, and spent several years in the Cubs' front office before being voted into Cooperstown in 1977.

Cool Papa Bell

Negro League legend "Cool Papa" Bell was a switch-hitter with tremendous power and amazing speed. Long-time teammate Satchel Paige said Bell could turn out the light and be in bed before the room got dark.

James Thomas Bell (1903-1991) moved at age 17 to St. Louis, where his mother felt he would get a good education. The St. Louis Stars signed him in 1922 as a knuckleball pitcher. Before being switched to the outfield, he earned his nickname by falling asleep before he was supposed to pitch. He was a "Cool Papa."

The popular Bell remained with the Stars for ten seasons, but gained his fame with the great Pittsburgh Crawfords and, later, with the Homestead Grays. In 1933 he joined the Crawfords, a team that raided other clubs to acquire future Hall of Famers Satchel Paige, Oscar Charleston, Judy Johnson, and Josh Gibson. Many other fine players toiled for the Crawfords at some time from '33 to 1936.

"Cool Papa" joined other Negro Leaguers playing in both the Dominican Republic and in Mexico. Bell was in such demand that he played for 29 summers and 21 winters. He was still hitting .300 at age 48, though fielding was no longer his strong suit. At times, his teams played three games in three towns in one day, traveling by bus.

Bell's lifetime average, by available records, was .338, and he hit .395 in exhibition games against major leaguers. He once stole over 175 bases in a 200-game season, but as he remembered, "one day I got five hits and stole five bases, but none of that was written down because they didn't bring the scorebook to the game that day." Happily, the Hall of Fame remembered enough to induct Bell in 1974.

BELL SLIDES EASILY INTO THIRD AT WASHINGTON'S GRIFFITH STADIUM.

Johnny Bench

Johnny Bench was the best offensive and defensive catcher of his time, and one of the best ever. The first player picked in the amateur draft to reach the Hall of Fame (in 1989), he had the greatest career of any National League receiver.

BENCH POWERED THE "BIG RED MACHINE" IN THE LATE 60S AND 70S.

Oklahoma-native Johnny Lee Bench (born 1947) was selected by Cincinnati in the second round of the 1965 draft and was named the 1966 Carolina League Player of the Year.

The Reds promoted Johnny in 1968, and he became the National League Rookie of the Year. Bench was a tremendously innovative defensive player, popularizing a one-handed catching method that allowed him greater mobility and easier use of his cannonlike arm. He was so overpowering that most baserunners would not challenge him.

Bench won two Most Valuable Player Awards and led the Reds to the post-season both years. In 1970, he was the youngest MVP ever, pacing the NL with 45 homers and 148 RBI. His second trophy came two years later, when Bench hit .270 with 40 round-trippers and 125 RBI.

The powerful "Big Red Machine" won consecutive World Series in 1975-76. In the fourth (and final) game of the 1976 World Series, Bench had two homers and five RBI, and hit .533 over the four games. He was voted the Series MVP.

Bench's 327 homers as a catcher were a record when he retired after the 1983 season, and his defensive statistics are still outstanding. He had 20 or more home runs in 11 seasons, played in 11 All-Star games, and won Gold Gloves from 1968 to 1977.

Yogi Berra

Yogi Berra was a mainstay of the most dominating baseball team in history, the New York Yankees from the end of World War II until the early 1960s. Although he never led the league in a single major offensive category, he won three Most Valuable Player Awards and played in a record fourteen World Series.

Lawrence Peter Berra (born 1925) grew up in St. Louis. He and childhood friend Joe Garagiola went to a Cardinal tryout in 1943 and Garagiola was offered $500 to sign, but Yogi was offered less. His pride hurt, Berra refused, and eventually signed with the Yankees. Before reaching the majors in 1946, he served with the Navy, and saw action in Normandy.

Once in New York, the likable Berra captured baseball fans' imaginations with his malapropisms. "It ain't over till it's over" has become a universal rallying cry. He was stocky and short, with a natural quality that fans found endearing. He was also one of the most dangerous hitters in the American League and worked hard to become a fine defensive player.

Yogi didn't become the Bombers' starting catcher until 1949. In 1950, he batted .322 with 28 homers and 124 RBI. Although his 1951 season wasn't as impressive (.294 average, 27 homers, and 88 RBI), he won his first MVP Award. He also won trophies in 1954 and '55, and it was a

BERRA WAS ONCE DESCRIBED BY MANAGER CASEY STENGEL AS "A PECULIAR FELLOW WITH AMAZING ABILITY."

tribute to his consistency that his three MVP seasons were not necessarily his best statistical years. He had 90 RBI in nine seasons, and slugged 20 or more homers 11 times.

Berra hit 358 homers in his career, which ended in 1963. He owns a host of World Series records, was an All-Star from 1948 to 1962, and managed the Yankees and the Mets to pennants. Yogi was inducted to the Hall of Fame in 1972.

Wade Boggs

No one in the 1980s and early 1990s reached base more consistently than Wade Boggs.

Wade Anthony Boggs, born in 1958 in Omaha, was drafted by the Boston Red Sox in 1976. He batted .263 in the New York-Penn League that year, the only time until 1992 that he hit under .300. Lacking power, Wade needed high averages to progress. When he won the 1981 International League batting title, the Red Sox promoted Boggs. When Boggs made the Red Sox in 1982, he played first and third base and batted .349 in 104 games. He won the third baseman's job the next season when Boston jettisoned incumbent Carney Lansford, who had won the AL batting crown the previous season.

From his rookie year through 1989, his worst average was .325. Boggs won AL batting titles five of his first seven seasons. He produced 200 or more hits seven consecutive times. Wade is the only man since Stan Musial in 1953 to total 200 or more hits and 100 or more walks in the same season. Boggs, a phenomenally disciplined batter, literally never swung at the first pitch or at balls out of the strike zone.

The hard-working Boggs devoted extra time to his defense. He used his good range and excellent reflexes to lead AL third basemen once in putouts and twice in double plays.

Eight times, Boggs hit 40 or more doubles in a season. He has paced the American League twice in two-baggers, twice in walks, and twice in runs scored. In 1987, he surprised the league with a career-high 24 homers.

In 1992, Boggs slumped to .259 and seven home runs. That winter, he left Boston to sign with the Yankees. He rebounded in 1993 to bat .302 with 74 walks. Boggs's career batting average and on-base percentage rank in the all-time top twenty, all but ensuring a spot in Cooperstown.

Lou Boudreau

Lou Boudreau was the best shortstop of the 1940s, a decade that produced several Hall of Famers at the position.

Louis Boudreau (born 1917) of Harvey, Illinois, played several sports in high school. The Cleveland Indians signed him in 1938, and he joined the Indians' Cedar Rapids farm club that year.

In 1939, Boudreau was in Cleveland to stay. In 1940, he hit .295 with 101 RBI. The next season he topped the AL in doubles. In 1944, Lou copped the AL batting crown, but was felled the next season by a broken ankle.

In 1942, Lou was named Cleveland's skipper. The "Boy Manager" quickly showed veteran maturity.

His leadership qualities included a remarkable self-confidence and a willingness to experiment.

Boudreau created the famous "Williams Shift" in 1946 to combat lefty pull-hitter Ted Williams. Lou moved to the right of second base, challenging Ted to hit the other way. He also converted strong-armed third baseman Bob Lemon into a pitcher.

When Bill Veeck bought the Indians in 1946, he wanted Boudreau to give up the manager's reins and concentrate solely on playing, but reconsidered when Cleveland fans protested. Veeck's patience paid off when the Tribe won the World Championship in 1948. Boudreau, the AL MVP, hit .355 that year and belted two homers in the tie-breaking playoff game with Boston.

Boudreau was one of the slowest infielders in the game, but he had a sure glove and great sense of anticipation. He led the AL in fielding percentage eight times in the 1940s.

Released by Cleveland in 1950, Lou joined the Red Sox, and became their skipper in 1952. He also managed the Athletics and Cubs and became a fixture in the Cubs' broadcast booth. Boudreau was elected to the Hall of Fame in 1970.

George Brett

One of the best third basemen of all time, George Brett led the expansion Royals' rise to glory on his way to 3,154 career hits.

In 1980, George Howard Brett (born 1953) came closer to batting .400 than any player since Ted Williams hit .406 in 1941. Brett ended with a .390 average, and was awarded the AL MVP Award. George led the Royals to the ALCS, which he iced with a mammoth three-run homer off Yankee ace Goose Gossage.

George, younger brother of former major-league pitcher Ken, was called up to Kansas City in 1974, where he remained for his entire 21-year career.

In 1975, Brett hit .308 and led the AL in hits and triples for the first of three times each. He won his first batting crown the next year with a .333 mark. The Royals won the AL West, but lost to the Yankees—a fate Kansas City also suffered the next two years.

The Royals won their first world championship in 1985. That season, Brett had 30 homers, 112 RBI, 103 walks, and a .335 average. He added three homers as the Royals rallied to beat Toronto in the playoffs. The Royals also came back to defeat St. Louis in the Series, with George batting .370 and scoring five runs.

George made headlines in the famous "Pine Tar Incident" in 1983, when Yankee manager Billy Martin protested Brett's game-winning home run because pine tar ran too far up his bat. Brett was called out, but the ruling was overturned.

Brett was also the first to win batting crowns in three different decades when he

A .305 LIFETIME HITTER, BRETT NEVER TOPPED .300 IN THE MINORS.

collected his third title in 1990 at age 37. He notched his 3,000th hit in 1992 and retired with a .305 lifetime average after hitting .266 with 19 homers for the 1993 Royals.

Lou Brock

On June 15, 1964, the Chicago Cubs traded promising outfielder Lou Brock to St. Louis. Brock hit .348 in Cardinal flannels to spark his team to a surprise NL pennant. He ruled left field in St. Louis for 15 more seasons before his 1985 election to the Hall of Fame.

Louis Clark Brock (born 1939) was a pitcher in high school, but switched to the outfield at Southern University in 1958. Signing with the Cubs in 1961, he led the Northern League with a .361 batting average and 117 runs scored, and joined the Cubs in 1962. He batted reasonably well in 1962-63, hitting .263 and .258, but poor defense led the Cubs to deal him.

Brock, an aggressive player, said, "Base-running arrogance is just like pitching arrogance or hitting arrogance... you have to instill that you are a force to the opposition."

Lou led the Cards to NL pennants in 1967-68, pacing the NL with 113 runs in '67 and smacking 21

IN ADDITION TO HIS **3,023** CAREER HITS, BROCK HAD **938** STOLEN BASES.

homers. In 1968, he led the National League with 46 doubles and 14 triples. In each of those World Series,

he hit over .400 and stole seven bases.

Brock led the NL in steals from 1966 to 1969, and from 1971 to 1974. (He finished second in 1970.) He led the NL with 126 runs scored in 1971. In 1974, Brock stole 118 bases, breaking Maury Wills's 1962 single-season mark of 104. His 893rd steal in 1977 shattered Ty Cobb's career record. Lou departed in style in '79, hitting .304 at age 40, earned his 3,000th hit, and stole 21 bases in 123 games.

He ended with 938 career steals, and was present when Rickey Henderson broke his single-season and career marks. Brock earned eight stolen base titles, scored 90 runs ten times, and hit over .300 eight years.

Dan Brouthers

Dan Brouthers was the greatest hitter of professional baseball's first two decades. He won five batting titles and at one time or another led his league in every major hitting department.

Dennis Joseph Brouthers (1858-1932) reached the National League in 1879. Originally a pitcher, he soon shifted to first base. Back in the NL in 1881 with Buffalo, Big Dan teamed with Deacon White, Hardy Richardson, and Jack Rowe to form an offensive force labeled "The Big Four." Brouthers led the NL in batting average, slugging average, and on-base percentage in both 1882 and 1883.

Financially strapped Buffalo sold the entire Big Four to Detroit in mid-September 1885 for $7,500. NL president Nick Young allowed the deal to stand only if the four did not play against pennant contenders. Due to this ruling, the Big Four missed the last three weeks of the season as all Detroit's remaining games were with teams in the race for the flag.

Playing a full schedule for Detroit in 1886, Brouthers led the league with 11 homers. The following season, his 153 runs scored, 36 doubles, and .426 on-base percentage (all league-leading figures) sparked the Wolverines to their only pennant. When Detroit folded in 1888 Brouthers was awarded to the Boston Beaneaters. The next year, Big Dan won his third batting crown. In 1890 and 1891, Brouthers played for flag-winning Boston clubs in the Players League and the American Association. He also played with the 1894 champion Orioles.

Brouthers served with a record nine different NL teams, the last being the New York Giants, for whom he played two games in 1904 at age 46. His .342 lifetime average is the eighth best in history, and the best ever for a first baseman. Brouthers was elected to the Hall of Fame in 1945.

Three Finger Brown

Three Finger Brown was one of a kind. He became a great pitcher because of, rather than in spite of, a crippling injury.

While visiting his uncle's farm, seven-year-old Mordecai Peter Centennial Brown (1876-1948) accidentally stuck his right hand under a corn chopper. Half of his index finger was torn off and the thumb and middle finger were permanently impaired.

The damaged hand hampered Brown in the field, but worked to his advantage when he turned to pitching. His unnatural grip caused straight pitches to behave like knuckleballs and made his curves significantly sharper. Ironically, Brown lacked a major-league fastball and might never have risen above semipro competition were it not for his uncle's corn chopper.

Brown joined the Cardinals in 1903, but St. Louis quickly dealt him to the Cubs. With Chicago, Brown instantly became the linchpin of Chicago's staff, and won 20 or more games six straight seasons beginning in 1906.

On June 13, 1905, Brown and Christy Mathewson of the Giants hooked up in one of the all-time great pitching duels. Brown surrendered just one hit but lost, 1-0, when Mathewson held the Cubs hitless. To Matty's dismay, it was his last win over Brown until 1909. In between, Brown topped Mathewson nine straight times.

Brown helped the Cubs win four pennants and two World Series between 1906 and 1910. In the 1908 World Series against Detroit, Brown tossed two shutouts. Two years earlier, Brown's 1.04 ERA set a 20th century NL record.

He spent 1914-15 in the Federal League, but returned to the Cubs in 1916. His final big-league appearance came that September against Mathewson, also making his final bow. Brown won 239 games, and his 2.06 career ERA is third on the all-time list. He died in 1948, one year before being elected to baseball's Hall of Fame.

Roy Campanella

Roy Campanella boosted the Dodgers of the 1950s into one of the top teams in baseball history. No catcher was a more complete performer than Campanella at his peak.

Born in Philadelphia, stocky Roy Campanella (1921-1993) played well enough as a youngster that by 1937, he was catching weekend games for the semipro Bacharach Giants. Campy soon joined the Baltimore Elite Giants, and by the mid-1940s, Campy challenged Josh Gibson as the best catcher in the Negro Leagues.

Campanella was approached by Brooklyn in 1945 but was unwilling to sign, thinking he would play with the Brooklyn Brown Dodgers Negro League team. Eventually, Campanella signed and spent 1946 with Nashua, where he was the Eastern League MVP. In 1947, at Montreal, he was the International League MVP.

An immediate success upon his arrival in Brooklyn in mid-1948, Campy had a rocket arm, a powerful bat, and handled pitchers well. In 1951, Campanella won the first of three Most Valuable Player Awards, batting .325 with 33 homers and 108 RBI.

His 1953 MVP season featured a league-leading 142 RBI, 41 homers, 103 runs scored, and a .312 average.

Campy chipped a bone in his left hand in spring training in 1954, and hit only .207. He rebounded in 1955 to win his third MVP by batting .318, with 32 homers and 107 RBI. His 1954 hand injury caused nerve damage, however, and his hitting declined.

He hoped for a return to form in 1958, but Campanella was paralyzed in a car crash in December 1957. Confined to a wheelchair, he continued to work for the Dodgers. Inducted to the Hall of Fame in 1969, Campy remarked, "You got to be a man to play baseball for a living, but you got to have a lot of little boy in you, too."

Rod Carew

In 1977, Rod Carew made a valiant run at the .400 mark, but fell just short. He topped .300 15 times and .330 ten times to win seven batting titles, posting over 200 hits in four seasons.

Born in the Panama Canal Zone in 1945, Rodney Scott Carew moved to New York at age 17. He joined the Twins' organization as a second baseman in 1964 and won AL Rookie of the Year honors in 1967 by hitting .292. He took his first batting title in 1969. Minnesota won the AL West in 1969 and 1970, but Carew and Co. ran into the Baltimore buzzsaw both years. Carew won batting titles each year from 1972 to 1975. Unfortunately, the slightly built Carew took a pounding at second. Twins manager Gene Mauch moved Rod to first base to extend his career. In 1977, he responded with his run at .400, which ended with a .388 mark, a league-leading 16 triples, 239 hits, and 128 runs. It was his sixth batting title. Carew was a runaway choice for the league's Most Valuable Player.

Rod was a master bunter—in 1972 he had 15 bunt-hits, but not a single home run—and astonished teammates by putting a handkerchief at various spots on the foul lines and dropping bunts onto it. In 1969, he stole home a record-tying seven times and swiped at least 20 sacks in seven seasons. He won his final batting title with a .333 mark in 1978, compiling 239 hits and 14 home runs.

In 1979, Carew was dealt to the California Angels.

CAREW'S MOVE TO CALIFORNIA IN 1979 BROUGHT THE ANGELS A DIVISION TITLE.

The 1979 Angels lost the ALCS, although Rod hit .412. In 1985, his final season, Carew hit .285, and became only the 16th man to collect 3,000 hits. He retired that fall with 3,053 safeties. In 1991, Carew was elected to Cooperstown in his first eligible year.

Steve Carlton

Tim McCarver, Steve Carlton's catcher, noted that Carlton "does not pitch to the hitter, he pitches through him. The batter hardly exists for Steve. He's playing an elevated form of catch."

In 1967, his first full season, Stephen Norman Carlton (born 1944) was 14-9 for the World Champion Cardinals. He broke through in 1969, notching a 17-11 record with a 2.17 ERA (second best in the NL). After a 20-9 record in 1971, the Cards dealt him to Philadelphia.

In 1972, Carlton totaled a 27-10 record, 310 strikeouts, and a 1.97 ERA for the last-place Phillies. "The Franchise" accounted for 46 percent of Philadelphia's 59 victories to set a modern record. He paced the NL in wins, ERA, starts, complete games, innings pitched, and strikeouts. Only Sandy Koufax had fanned 300 in the NL before Carlton. That year, Carlton captured his first Cy Young Award.

Philadelphia won the NL East in 1976 as Carlton was

CARLTON'S WICKED SLIDER EARNED HIM SEVEN ALL-STAR SELECTIONS.

20-7. He won his second Cy Young Award in 1977, with a 23-10 record, as the Phils won another division title. It took a league-leading 24 wins from Carlton in 1980 to send the Phillies to their first World Series in 30 years. He won his third Cy Young Award, striking out a league-best 286 batters.

Carlton took an unprecedented fourth Cy Young in 1982, finishing 23-11 with league highs in strikeouts and innings pitched. Age and injury blunted Steve's wicked slider, and he retired in 1988. His 329 victories are ninth on the all-time list.

Over his career, Carlton accumulated six 20-win seasons and led the NL in strikeouts five times and wins four times. Second on the career list with 4,136 Ks, Carlton was fittingly inducted into the Hall of Fame in 1994.

Gary Carter

Gary Carter helped the Mets over the top in the mid-1980s. In order to challenge for an NL East title, they needed another big hitter and a capable catcher to guide their talented but inexperienced pitching staff. Before the 1985 season, New York shipped four players to Montreal for Carter, who promptly hit .281 with 32 home runs and led National League catchers in

putouts and chances per game.

Another superb season by Carter in 1986 helped the Mets win a divisional crown. The Mets finished 108-54, while Carter's 24 homers and 105 RBI led New York to a world title, defeating Boston in seven.

Gary Edmund Carter (born 1954) began his major-league career in 1975 as an outfielder, batting .270 with 17 homers and 68 RBI. By 1977, his part-time play behind the plate was so inspired that the Expos gave the starting job to Carter that June.

The vote of confidence inspired Carter, who hit .284 with 31 homers and 84 RBI, and proved he could be a full-time major-league catcher by pacing NL backstops in assists, putouts, and double plays. In 1979, he batted .283 with 22 more four-baggers, and again led league catchers in assists, putouts, and double plays.

The Expos finished second in 1980, led by Carter's 29 homers and 101 RBI. He led NL catchers in putouts, assists, and fielding percentage. Carter hit .293 with 29 homers and 97 RBI in 1982. In 1984, he batted .294 with 27 homers and a league-leading 106 RBI before being dealt to the Mets.

In 1992, he returned to Montreal and closed out his great career. Carter hit 319 lifetime home runs and was a fiery and inspiring field leader. Nobody worked harder than Gary Carter.

Oscar Charleston put punch in the lineups of a dozen teams in his 35-year career. A barrel-chested man of great strength, he hit for power and average and ran like the wind. Only Josh Gibson challenges Oscar's reputation as a slugger, and only "Cool Papa" Bell is mentioned with him when top Negro League center fielders are named.

Born in Indianapolis, Oscar McKinley Charleston (1896-1954) began his career in 1912 in the Philippines as a member of the Army. Discharged in 1915, Charleston signed with the Indianapolis ABCs.

John B. Holway wrote "there were three things Oscar Charleston excelled at on the field: hitting, fielding, and fighting. He loved all three, and it's a toss-up which he was best at." Each of the three is documented. Charleston's lifetime average is .357. Charleston's 11 homers against major-league pitchers in exhibition games ties for the highest recorded total. In the

CHARLESTON LED THE INDIANAPOLIS CLOWNS TO A CHAMPIONSHIP IN 1954.

field, Oscar was just as impressive, with an arm more accurate than strong, and the speed to run down drives in any part of the park easily.

Infielders got out of Oscar's way as he ran the bases; Charleston had considerable strength, speed, and a mean streak. Off the field he was just as formidable, ripping the hood off a Florida Klansman in 1935. Charleston resembled Babe Ruth in his love for women and the good life. Like the Babe, Oscar is remembered as genial and good-natured, though few were blind to his faults.

Charleston stayed on past his prime as a player-manager, mainly with the Pittsburgh Crawfords. He switched to first base after a chronic weight problem got the best of him. Charleston's legacy was finally honored by the Hall of Fame in 1976.

Roger Clemens

Roger Clemens was the finest pitcher in baseball during the late 1980s and early 1990s. Despite pitching in small Fenway Park, he won three Cy Young Awards.

William Roger Clemens (born 1962) attended the University of Texas, where he helped the Longhorns win the 1983 NCAA Championship. That year, he was a first-round pick of the Red Sox.

Boston promoted him in 1984 and, despite a forearm injury, he went 9-4. In 1985, Clemens was hampered by a bad shoulder, but still went 7-5 with a 3.29 ERA.

Clemens returned healthy in 1986 and helped Boston to its first World Series in a decade. He had a 24-4 record with 10 complete games, 238 strikeouts, and a league-best 2.48 ERA. He also set a single-game major-league record by striking out 20 Mariners in Fenway Park on April 29. Clemens was named the Cy Young winner and the AL MVP.

CLEMENS WAS THE POWER PITCHER OF NOTE IN THE LATE 1980S

In 1987, Clemens became the first Red Sox pitcher with back-to-back 20-win seasons in 15 years. He paced the league in wins, winning percentage, complete games, and shutouts and again was the Cy Young winner.

A late-season slump stopped Clemens from a third straight 20-win season in 1988. However, he did lead the American League with 291 strikeouts. In 1990, Clemens led the Red Sox to the ALCS again with a 21-6 record and a 1.93 ERA. The next season, Clemens's 2.62 ERA and 241 strikeouts again led the league, and he won his third Cy Young Award. 1992 saw a third-straight ERA crown, and Clemens also led the American League in shutouts for the fifth time.

Clemens's peak performance already guarantees him entry to the Hall of Fame.

Roberto Clemente

Roberto Clemente once said, "A country without idols is nothing." Clemente was an idol to many people in many countries. He owned one of the strongest outfield arms ever, won four batting titles, and had 3,000 hits.

Roberto Clemente y Walker (1934-1973) grew up near San Juan, Puerto Rico. He played for a pennant-winning Santurce team in 1952, and the next year, his outfield mate was Willie Mays. In 1954,

ROBERTO CLEMENTE PICKS UP CAREER HIT NUMBER 3,000, ALSO HIS LAST.

Clemente signed with the Dodgers, who played him sparingly. The Pirates drafted him in 1955.

By 1960, Clemente had emerged as a star, achieving personal bests in runs, home runs, RBI, and batting average. He hit .310 as the Pirates won the World Series, then raised his game another notch in 1961, hitting .351, the first of five times he batted above .340. Roberto won four batting titles, hit 240 homers, and was the National League MVP in 1966.

Clemente's arm was a deadly cannon that he unleashed from impossible angles and distances. The power and accuracy with which he threw is legendary. He won Gold

Gloves every year from 1961 through 1972 and played more games in right field than anyone else in NL history.

Although Clemente suffered from a myriad of injuries throughout his career, he posted the top batting average of the 1960s at .328. Clemente batted .312 in 1972, at age 38, and rapped his 3,000th hit on September 30th. Sadly, it was his last.

On December 31, 1972, he was on a plane airlifting relief supplies to earthquake-torn Nicaragua. The plane crashed near the Puerto Rico coast; there were no survivors. Clemente was voted into the Hall of Fame in an extraordinary special election held just 11 weeks after his death.

Ty Cobb

When the first Hall of Fame vote was taken in 1936, Ty Cobb was the top vote-getter, named on 222 of the 226 ballots cast. The shock was not that "The Georgia Peach" outpolled every other player, but that four voters ignored Cobb. Of course, Cobb was not just one of the greatest players ever, he 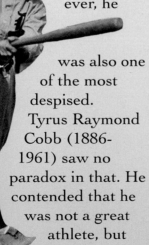 was also one of the most despised.

Tyrus Raymond Cobb (1886-1961) saw no paradox in that. He contended that he was not a great athlete, but became a great player due to an unparalleled desire to win. His hostile, suspicious nature and reckless slides with spikes high meant Cobb was shunned by other players.

When he retired after 24 big-league seasons, Cobb held almost every major batting and base-running record.

Cobb won ten batting titles, led the league in runs scored five times, RBI four times, slugging percentage eight times, and on-base percentage six times. His totals of 4,191 hits and 892 stolen bases are the second- and third-highest totals ever. Cobb was the dominant player of his day, but to his regret, never played on a World Series winner.

He was fired as the Tigers player-manager following the 1926 season after it was discovered that he and Tris Speaker had apparently rigged a 1919 game. It was

COBB'S CAREER BATTING AVERAGE (.366) IS STILL TOPS.

foreordained that Detroit would win; Cobb wouldn't ever agree to finish less than first in anything.

Cobb signed with the Philadelphia Athletics and retired after the 1928 season. For the next 33 years he lived on the terms under which he had played—comfortable, but essentially alone.

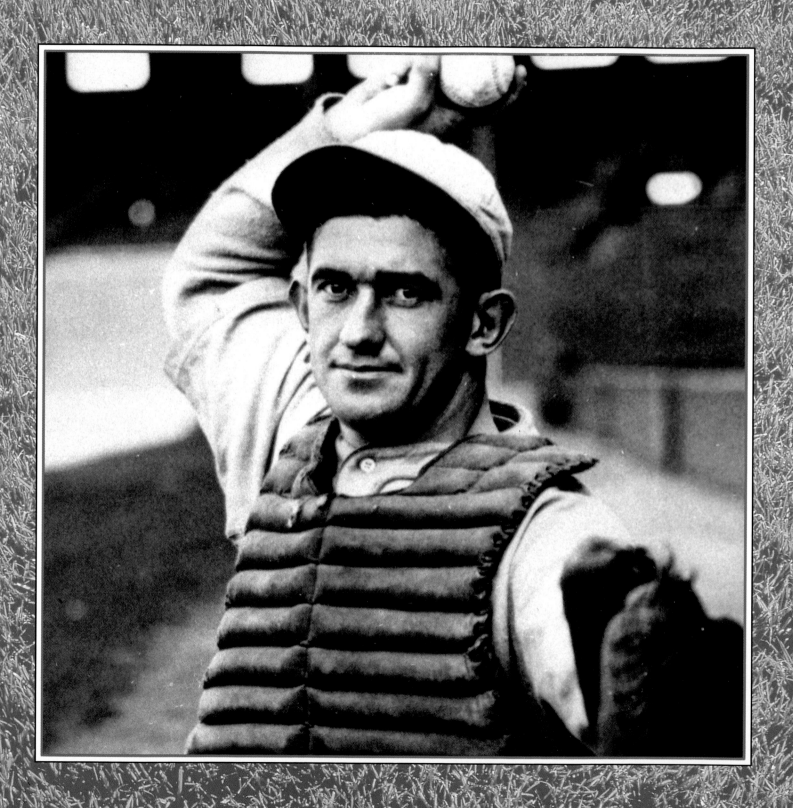

Mickey Cochrane

Mickey Cochrane was, throughout his career, the best-hitting catcher in baseball. His .320 batting average and .419 on-base percentage are career records for a catcher. Cochrane also had an exceptional batting eye, and walked four times as often as he struck out.

In 1923, Gordon Stanley Cochrane (1903-1962) signed his first minor-league contract under an assumed name, not to protect his college eligibility—he had already been a five-sport star at Boston University—but to guard his ego.

Cochrane did well, although it took him several weeks to adjust to his new position behind the plate. Soon, he caught the eye of Connie Mack, who took over Portland in the Pacific Coast League just to give Mickey his own place to hone his skills.

Joining the Mackmen in 1925, Cochrane caught a rookie-record 134 games and hit .331. In 1929, he batted .331 with 69 walks and just eight strikeouts. Mickey was far from a polished maskman, however, and some felt that he never fully mastered his trade. When Pepper Martin ran wild for the Cardinals against the A's in the 1931 World Series, Philadelphia pitcher George Earnshaw publicly blamed Cochrane.

Mickey played on five pennant winners—three in Philadelphia and two more after he was traded to Detroit in 1933. He had early success as a player-manager, winning flags in 1934 and 1935.

On May 25, 1937, Mickey was beaned by New York's Bump Hadley and hovered near death for over a week before recovering. Detroit owner Walter Briggs forbade Cochrane to play again after doctors warned a second beaning could be fatal. Through as a player, Mickey managed the Tigers another one and one-half seasons. He also served in the front offices of the A's and Tigers before being named to the Hall of Fame in 1947.

Eddie Collins

John McGraw once said that Eddie Collins was the best ballplayer he'd ever seen, and Connie Mack called Collins the best second baseman he saw—strong endorsements from two men who watched a lot of baseball. Collins played 25 seasons, turning in one outstanding campaign after another, and is arguably the best second baseman ever.

Edward Trowbridge Collins (1887-1951) joined Mack's Philadelphia Athletics after college and was one-quarter of the famous "$100,000 Infield." In 1910, he stole a then-record 81 bases. He was part of the three championship teams in Philly.

When the Athletics were broken up after 1914, Collins, that year's AL MVP, was sold to the White Sox for a record $50,000. "Cocky" led the Sox to a World Series triumph in 1917. One of the 1919 "Clean Sox," Eddie never forgave the eight players who sold out.

COLLINS HAD IT ALL—FIELDING, HITTING, AND BASESTEALING

Collins did not have much power, but played when power was not a major part of the game. He owns a .333 lifetime batting average and a .406 career on-base percentage. He hit over .340 ten times, collecting 3,311 hits, and almost never struck out. Collins owns many second sacker fielding records, including most putouts, assists, and total chances. Few have matched Eddie's abilities and longevity. His skill at adapting his style of play to the changing style of baseball may have been his greatest asset.

Collins was named player-manager of the White Sox in 1924 but never finished higher than fifth in his two years at the helm. He retired from playing in 1930. Later, as general manager of the Red Sox, Collins signed future greats Ted Williams and Bobby Doerr. The Hall of Fame enshrined Eddie in 1939.

Jimmy Collins

By 1908, when Home Run Baker debuted with the Philadelphia Athletics, major-league baseball had existed for 36 seasons; only one third baseman who played before Baker's time is in the Hall of Fame. Jimmy Collins, elected in 1945, was the finest third sacker of the nineteenth century.

Those who witnessed James Joseph Collins (1870-1943) play claimed he was without even a close rival. The first to charge bunts and play them bare-handed, he also ranged equally well toward the line or to his left. Playing for Boston in 1899, he accepted a record 593 chances. The following year, he set a 20th century mark with 251 putouts. Until the 1940s, third base was seen primarily as a defensive position; his glove alone made Collins a star.

Adding more weight to his credentials, Collins was also a productive hitter and a fine manager. Posting a lifetime average of .294, Collins led the NL with 15 homers in 1898 and drove in 90 or more runs five straight times. He piloted the Boston Pilgrims to the championship in the first modern World Series in 1903, then garnered a second pennant the next year.

Collins's baseball success was anything but immediate. He didn't reach the majors, with Boston, until 1895. Beginning in 1896, he held down the hot corner for the Beaneaters for five seasons. However, in 1901, Collins grabbed an offer from the Boston team in the new American League. Collins's theft caused the AL club to be called the "Invaders" initially.

As the manager and third baseman of the new Hub entry, Collins surrendered the former post late in 1906. The BoSox soon dealt Collins to the Athletics. After hitting just .217 in 1908, he was released by Philadelphia and replaced by none other than the sweet-swinging Home Run Baker. This is the only time in history that one future Hall of Fame third baseman was succeeded by another.

Sam Crawford

In Sam Crawford's time, the great sluggers hit triples, not home runs. By that standard, Crawford was the dead-ball era's biggest power threat. He left the majors in 1917 with 309 triples, still the major-league record. Crawford is also the only player in this century to lead both major leagues in home runs.

Born in Wahoo, Nebraska, Samuel Earl Crawford (1880-1968) played his first pro baseball in 1899 and did so well that Cincinnati purchased him late that season. Still just 19 years old when he debuted with the Reds, Crawford hit .307 with eight triples in 31 games.

After the 1902 season, Crawford escaped the lowly Reds, a cellar finisher in 1901 despite his loop-leading 16 homers. Jumping to Detroit in the American League, he hit .335 in his first AL season with 25 triples. Even with Crawford's slugging, Detroit remained a second-division team until Ty Cobb came along in 1905. Playing side by side in the outfield, the pair spearheaded the

"Wahoo Sam Crawford holds the Major-League record for triples with 309 lifetime."

1907 to 1909 Tigers, the first team in American League history to garner three consecutive pennants.

Crawford fashioned a .309 career batting average and logged at least ten triples in every full season he played. He was a loop leader in three-baggers six times and also topped the AL in RBI on three occasions.

During his 14-year tour of duty with Detroit, Crawford became very popular. This made Cobb jealous, and relations between the two deteriorated. Soon, they only spoke when calling each other off fly balls. Ironically, Ty Cobb campaigned the hardest for Crawford when he was passed over for selection to the Hall of Fame. In 1957, Crawford received the long-overdue honor.

Joe Cronin

At age 20 in 1926, Joe Cronin sat on the bench, was farmed out, and then sold. In 1959, he became president of the American League. Between, he turned in a Hall of Fame career as a great offensive shortstop.

Joseph Edward Cronin (1906-1984) was born in San Francisco a few months after the great earthquake. Joe was a star high school athlete and played semi-pro ball after graduation. A Pittsburgh scout signed Joe in 1925, and after a good season with Johnstown in the Mid-Atlantic League, Cronin was promoted to the Pirates. He then sat behind Glenn Wright for two seasons.

Cronin moved to the AL, landing in Washington in 1928. He had a decent campaign in 1929, and followed it up with a *Sporting News* MVP season in 1930. He hit .346 with 127 runs scored and 126 RBI. Joe totaled 100 RBI a remarkable eight times. Cronin compiled a lifetime .301 batting average, hitting over .300 in 11 seasons. He socked 51 doubles in 1938, and hit 515 in his career. Both for his bat and his outstanding defensive ability, he was named outstanding major-league shortstop by *The Sporting News* seven times.

Active in an era when player-managers were common, he served a long term in that role. Cronin ran the Senators in 1933-34, and skippered the Red Sox from 1935 to '47 after Boston purchased him. His debut season as manager produced a pennant in 1933, and he hit .318 in that fall's World Series. Ted Williams said in 1946 that Cronin was "the greatest manager I ever played for." Cronin, ironically, had doubts about his double duty and tried to resign back in 1933. He finished first again in 1946, the year he retired as a player, and brought Boston its first pennant since 1918.

In 1959, Joe was the first former player to be elected AL president. During his tenure, he oversaw the league's growth from eight to 12 teams and was instrumental in formulating divisional play. He remained in office until 1973, then assumed the post of AL chairman.

Dizzy Dean

One of the most entertaining players ever, Dizzy Dean blazed bright in baseball's sky for five seasons. He was the last NL pitcher to win 30 games in a season, was the league's Most Valuable Player in 1934, and finished second in the voting in 1935 and 1936.

Jay Hanna Dean (1911-1974) honed his pitching skills—and got his nickname—in the Army, and a Cardinals scout signed him in 1930. Dean was 25-10 that year in the minors and tossed a three-hit shutout for the Cardinals on the final day of the season. He was summoned by St. Louis in 1932 and won 18 games, led the NL in shutouts and innings pitched, and won his first of four straight strikeout titles for the fun-loving "Gashouse Gang."

Dizzy was a natural clown but also a shrewd negotiator. He staged a holdout during the 1934 season for his brother, and fellow Redbirds pitcher, Paul, who Diz felt was underpaid. Despite missing some starts, the elder Dean went 30-7, and Paul was 19-11.

The Deans won all of the Cardinals' World Series games that year. While pinch-running in game four, Dizzy was hit in the forehead by a throw. Some feared a serious injury, but the next day's headlines read "X-Ray of Dean's Head Reveals Nothing." Dizzy pitched a shutout in the deciding seventh game.

During the 1937 All-Star game, a line drive broke

DEAN (LEFT) IS THE LAST PITCHER TO POST 30 WINS IN A SEASON.

Dizzy's toe. He came back too soon, and in doing so altered his motion, which injured his right arm. He never fully recovered, and retired in 1941 at age 30 with 150 career victories. Hall of Fame honors followed in 1953.

E d D elahanty

Some consider Ed Delahanty the greatest righthanded hitter of all time. He batted over .400 three times and was the only player to win batting titles in both the National League and American League. Yet Delahanty is one of baseball's most tragic figures.

Born in Cleveland, Edward James Delahanty (1867-1903) broke in with Philadelphia in 1888. Allowed to play the outfield full-time in 1892, he had his first good year, batting .306, and never again hit below .323.

"Big Ed" played for the Phillies for 13 of his first 14 seasons (he spent 1890 with Cleveland of the Players League). With Delahanty in left field, Philadelphia had the strongest attack in major-league baseball between 1891 and 1894.

Delahanty led the NL in almost every major hitting

"BIG ED" PACED THE NL FOUR TIMES IN DOUBLES AND SLUGGING FOR HIS ALSO-RAN PHILLIES.

department at least once. In 1899, while rapping .410 and leading the loop in hits and RBI, Delahanty ripped 55 doubles—a mark that stood until 1923.

In 1901, Delahanty signed with Washington of the American League. The following year, Big Ed captured the AL hitting crown when he stroked .376.

Delahanty still longed to join a pennant winner. Before the 1903 season he struck a deal with the New York Giants, but a peace settlement between the two leagues froze all players with their old teams. Stuck in Washington, and experiencing marital trouble, Delahanty began drinking heavily. On the night of July 2, 1903, he was ejected from a train near Niagara Falls. Drunk and frustrated, he ran after the locomotive but slipped on the train tracks and plunged to his death into the Niagara River. In 1945, Delahanty, owner of a .346 lifetime average, was named to the Hall of Fame.

Bill Dickey

Until Yogi Berra came along, Bill Dickey was the greatest Yankee catcher. The finest backstop of his time, he joined the Hall of Fame in 1954.

Born in Bastrop, Louisiana, William Malcolm Dickey (1907-1993) batted .324 in his first full major-league season as a Yankee. He was Lou Gehrig's roommate, and they were a matched set—quiet and consistent. Dickey topped the .300 mark ten times, and his .362 average in 1936 is a record for backstops. From 1936 to 1939, the lefthanded Dickey, aided by a short right field porch in Yankee Stadium, popped over 20 homers a year.

A hard worker and a fierce competitor, Dickey

BILL DICKEY GUIDED THE GREAT YANKEE TEAMS OF THE 30'S AND 40'S

handled Yankee pitching staffs for seven World Series championships. His 17-year career spanned the Ruth and DiMaggio eras. Bill caught 100 or more games for 13 consecutive seasons, a record that stood until Johnny Bench appeared. At the time of Dickey's retirement, he held the records for putouts and fielding average.

Although generally calm on the field, Bill lost his cool one day in 1932,

receiving a one-month suspension and a fine after breaking baserunner Carl Reynolds's jaw with one punch after a collision at home plate. In 1943, Dickey's two-run homer in the fifth and final World Series game that fall propelled the Yanks to the championship.

Bill then enlisted in the Navy, missing the 1944 and 1945 seasons. He finished his career in 1946. When the Bombers were working in a young kid named Berra, Bill was called in to show the youngster how to do it.

Martin Dihigo

Since Negro League teams obtained slender profit margins, squads often consisted of 14 to 18 players. The most valuable player was usually the one who played several positions. Martin Dihigo could pitch and play seven positions (all but catcher) at an All-Star level.

Born in Matanzas, Cuba, Martin Dihigo (1905-1971) began his pro career in 1923 in the Cuban Winter League as a 17-year-old strong-armed, weak-hitting outfielder. Legend has it he won a distance-throwing contest against a jai alai player who was allowed to use his wicker-basket *cesta*. He is compared to Roberto Clemente by those who saw both players throw.

Like many Negro Leaguers, Martin played all over North, Central, and South America in his career. Unlike most, he starred almost everywhere he saw action.

From the time he came to America (in 1923) through 1936, he made only occasional forays to the pitching mound, but Dihigo pitched more often when he played in Latin America. His pitching stats include an 18-2 record and an 0.90 ERA in 1938, and a 22-7 record and a 2.53 ERA in 1942. He twirled the first no-hitter in Mexican League history. According to the latest available records, he won 256 games while dropping only 136.

Martin developed into a great hitter by age 20. He hit over .400 three times, led two different leagues in batting average, and slugged a 500-foot round-tripper in 1936. Dihigo paced his league in homers in 1926 and in 1935. He posted a .316 career average in the Negro Leagues between 1923 and 1945.

In the field, he tossed out runners at home plate with frightening regularity. Dihigo often pitched in relief, especially as a manager. He threw no-hitters in Venezuela, Puerto Rico, as well as Mexico, and skippered professional clubs in America, Mexico, and Cuba until 1950.

After his retirement, Dihigo became a broadcaster and Cuba's Minister of Sport. Martin is the only player in the Cuban, Mexican, and American Halls of Fame.

Joe DiMaggio

If Joe DiMaggio wasn't the greatest all-around player in baseball history, he almost certainly was the most majestic.

Joseph Paul DiMaggio (born 1914) and his brothers Vince and Dom played baseball on the San Francisco sandlots hour after hour. In 1932, Joe signed with the San Francisco Seals. In 1933, a .340 batting average, 28 homers, and 169 RBI made him a local hero.

DiMaggio batted .341 in 1934, and the Yankees paid $25,000 and five players for Joe. Assigned back to San Francisco for 1935, DiMag batted .398 with 34 homers and 154 RBI.

DiMaggio hit it big in Gotham in 1936, helping the Yankees to the first of four consecutive World Championships. Although hampered by Yankee Stadium's cavernous left field, the Yankee Clipper twice led the AL in homers and twice in slugging. He was fast, strong, and smart on the field.

Joltin' Joe played center with grace and threw with terrific power. He paced

DiMAGGIO'S 56-GAME HITTING STREAK HAS NEVER BEEN MATCHED.

the league with 22 assists in 1936, then notched totals of 21 and 20 before opponents stopped running on him.

He won his first MVP Award in 1939 with a career-best .381 average. When he won his second trophy in 1941, he had 76 walks and only 13 strikeouts. DiMaggio also hit in a record 56 consecutive games, a feat that has never been matched.

World War II deprived Joe of three seasons. In 1947, he won his third MVP and the Yankees won another Championship. A heel injury slowed Joe in 1948. He returned in 1949 to help the Yankees win the first of five straight World titles, but injuries and the grind of the road led DiMaggio to retire after the 1951 season.

Buck Ewing

William Buckingham Ewing's statistics seem noteworthy but hardly extraordinary. He led the National League in home runs in 1883 and in triples in 1884, but his career accomplishments appear modest. In Ewing's case, however, statistics deceive. In 1919, famed sportswriter Francis Richter deemed Ewing, Ty Cobb, and Honus Wagner the three greatest players in baseball history, and stated that Ewing might have been the best of all—"a player without a weakness of any kind, physical, mental, or temperamental."

Ewing (1859-1906) hit just .250 with Troy in 1881, his first full big-league season. Eventually, he became a speedy and sometimes powerful leadoff hitter, and from the outset of his 18-year career was viewed as a peerless defensive catcher and field leader.

He was one of the first to catalogue opposing batters' weaknesses during pre-game clubhouse meetings. John Foster wrote that "as a thrower to bases, Ewing never had a superior...it was said, 'he handed the ball to the second baseman from the batter's box.'"

Catchers in the 1800s seldom worked more than half their team's games. While most backstops simply took frequent days off, Ewing was good enough to fill in anywhere on the diamond. In 1889, with the Giants fighting for the pennant, Ewing even pitched two complete-game victories.

He jumped to the Players League the following year and was named player-manager of the New York Giants.

Ewing finished his playing career for Cincy in 1897 with a .303 lifetime average. He succumbed to diabetes on October 20, 1906. In 1936, Buck tied for first place in the initial vote of the old-timers for the Hall of Fame.

Bob Feller

Bob Feller was probably harmed more than any other great player by World War II. Had Feller's career proceeded without interruption, instead of losing nearly four full seasons, he might be considered the greatest pitcher in history.

Born in 1918 in Iowa, Robert William Andrew Feller was signed by Cleveland in 1935 while still in high school. The signing was illegal according to the rules of the time, but Commissioner Kenesaw Mountain Landis feared a bidding war among the other teams if Feller was made a free agent, and let the deal stand.

He debuted with Cleveland in a July 1936 exhibition game against the Cardinals. Though only 17, Feller fanned eight Redbirds in the three innings he hurled. Plate umpire Bob Ormsby labeled Feller the fastest pitcher he had ever seen.

However, batters learned that while Feller was unhittable, they could simply wait for walks. In 1938, he topped the majors with 240 strikeouts and set a modern single-game record with 18 Ks. However, he also allowed 208 walks.

His control improving, Feller paced the American League in wins during each of the next three seasons before entering the Navy. In 1940, Feller tossed the first Opening Day no-hitter in AL history and helped the Tribe finish second that year.

Returning from the war, Feller had his finest season in 1946 with 26 wins and 348 strikeouts. He continued as one of the game's top hurlers until 1955.

FELLER LED THE AMERICAN LEAGUE IN STRIKEOUTS SEVEN TIMES.

The author of three career no-hitters and 12 one-hit games, Feller was elected to the Hall of Fame in 1962.

Rollie Fingers

After promoting Rollie Fingers from the minors in 1969, the A's shuttled him between starting and the bullpen. Finally in 1971, Oakland manager Dick Williams decided Fingers was best suited for relief work. He responded with 17 saves that year and 21 in 1972. As baseball's first superstar career reliever, Fingers redefined the closer's role.

Clean shaven when he reached the majors, Roland Glen Fingers (born 1946) soon grew the longest mustache, tip to tip, in major-league history. His career high-point came in the 1974 World Series against the Dodgers. With the A's shooting for their third World Championship in a row, Fingers won the first game of the Series and then

saved the final two contests. For his efforts, Fingers earned Series MVP honors.

After two more seasons, Rollie became a free agent and signed a five-year deal with the Padres. In each of his first two seasons in San Diego, he topped the NL in saves. In 1980, Fingers was swapped to the Cardinals

FINGERS'S PITCHING PERFORMANCE DEFINED THE ROLE OF THE "CLOSER."

and then immediately shipped to Milwaukee in the year's biggest deal.

Fingers's finest season was the strike-abbreviated 1981 campaign. In 47 appearances, he collected a major league-leading 28 saves and etched a 1.04 ERA. His banner year garnered him the MVP and the Cy Young Awards. When the Brewers won their first pennant in 1982, an ailing elbow kept Fingers out of their World Series loss to the Cardinals.

Elbow problems shelved Fingers all of 1983, but he posted 23 saves in 1984 and a 1.96 ERA. The 1985 campaign proved to be his last, however, when a back injury led to a 1-6 record. Fingers and his 341 career saves were voted to the Hall of Fame in 1992.

Carlton Fisk

Carlton Fisk retired with records for games caught and home runs by a catcher, but is best remembered for his game-winning home run in the sixth game of the 1975 World Series.

In that game, the Reds and the Red Sox were tied in the bottom of the 12th inning when Fisk stepped to the plate. The image of

Fisk swinging, watching the ball sail, and waving his arms to encourage it to stay fair, is truly memorable.

Carlton Ernest Fisk (born 1947) was drafted by the Boston Red Sox in 1967 and began his pro career the next year. Fisk cracked the Red Sox lineup in 1972, leading the AL with nine triples. His play earned him American League Rookie of the Year honors.

In 1973 Carlton slammed 26 homers, but missed most of 1974 and some of 1975 with injuries. Following a subpar 1976 season, Fisk rebounded in 1977 to hit .315 with 26 homers and 103 RBI.

After the 1980 season, Fisk became a free agent and signed with the White Sox. Chicago was desperate both for offense and for an on-field general with major-league experience.

He helped the Sox to a 1983 division title, hitting .289 with 26 homers and 86 RBI. Plagued by injuries in 1984, he still had 21 homers. The next season, he returned with career highs in homers (37) and RBI (107). He credited his comeback to an extensive training program, which he maintained the rest of his career.

In 1990 Fisk smashed Johnny Bench's mark of most homers by a catcher; in 1993 Carlton broke Bob Boone's record for most games caught. Shortly afterward, the White Sox released him, and Fisk retired with 376 career round-trippers and a .269 average.

Whitey Ford

The "Chairman of the Board" was the ace of the 1950s Yankees' staff. His .690 winning percentage is the best of any modern 200-game winner. Ford's teams won 11 pennants and seven World Series, helped largely by Whitey's streak of 33 scoreless Series innings.

Edward Charles Ford (born 1926) of New York City started pitching only as a senior in high school.

FORD PITCHED MORE GAMES IN WORLD SERIES PLAY THAN ANYONE.

He started his pro career in 1947 with a 13-4 record and led the Eastern League with a 1.61 ERA in 1949.

Summoned to New York in mid-1950, he went 9-1 in 12 starts and tossed a shutout in that fall's World Series. He served two years in the military, then returned in 1953 with an 18-6 mark to help the Yankees win their fifth straight World Championship.

Whitey didn't just win, he won often. In 12 seasons, he was at least six games over .500. He led the AL with 18 wins in 1955 and a 2.47 ERA in 1956. Yankee Manager Casey Stengel usually used Ford only against good teams and refused to overwork his star.

When Ralph Houk took the Yankee reins in 1961, he unleashed Whitey, who responded with a 25-4 record in a league-high 39 starts to win the Cy Young Award. In 1963, he was 24-7, leading the AL in starts and innings pitched.

Ford used several pitches, most of them legal. The threat of his spitball kept hitters guessing, and may have helped him more than the actual pitch itself.

Whitey, his buddy Mickey Mantle, and other Yankees loved the night life. "When Whitey pitched, he always felt like unwinding that night after the ballgame," Mantle said. (He added that he, too, was ready to celebrate if Whitey won.) Ford, his 236 wins, and Mantle all joined the Hall of Fame in 1974.

Jimmy Foxx

In an era of big hitters, Jimmie Foxx won four home run titles and two batting titles. He was the first American Leaguer to win consecutive MVP Awards and the first three-time winner.

James Emory Foxx (1907-1967) grew up in rural Maryland. "Home Run" Baker scouted Foxx in high school. Jimmie signed a contract at age 16. Both the Yankees and Athletics were interested in Foxx, but Baker steered Jimmie to the A's as a favor to Connie Mack.

Foxx initially joined Philadelphia in 1924, and from 1926 to 1928 filled in at catcher, first, and third.

By the time Foxx became the regular first baseman in 1929, the A's were a powerhouse. "Double X" appeared in three consecutive World Series from 1929 to 1931 (his only trips to the Fall Classic). Foxx and Al Simmons combined for 192 home runs in those three years, and Lefty Grove was 79-15. Jimmie won consecutive MVPs in 1932 and '33. He had 58 homers and 169 RBI in 1932, and he earned the Triple Crown in 1933 with 48 homers, 163 RBI, and a .356 average. He hit .344 and slugged .609 in 18 World Series games.

Mack sold Foxx to Boston in 1936, and Jimmie hailed his arrival by hitting 41 homers and 143 RBI.

Foxx was a drinker, but he had enough left for a final burst. After "slumping" to 36 homers, 127 RBI, and a career-low .285 average in 1937, he bounced back in 1938 to hit 50 homers and lead the AL in RBI and average to win his third MVP Award.

THE BURLY FOXX HIT 30 OR MORE HOMERS FOR 12 SEASONS, A MAJOR-LEAGUE RECORD.

Appendicitis shortened his terrific 1939 season, and 1940 was his last productive year as he totaled 36 home runs. When Foxx retired in 1945, only Babe Ruth had more home runs. He was named to the Hall of Fame in 1951.

Frankie Frisch

Frankie Frisch was a driven, highly competitive player. There could be only one leader on a team managed by John McGraw, but McGraw knew "The Fordham Flash" could help the New York Giants. In 1919, Frank Francis Frisch (1898-1973) joined the club, and the Giants won NL flags from 1921 to 1925, and New York won world titles in 1921 and 1922. Frisch hit .341 and .327, respectively, those two years. He also wowed baseball fans with his slick fielding.

In fact, *The New York Times* called him "possibly the flashiest second baseman of any day." In 1923, he paced the league with 223 hits and began to establish himself as a star. The next season, he led the NL by scoring 121 runs, while garnering 198 hits.

Although he played in the lively ball era, Frisch never hit more than a dozen home runs in a season. However, he hit over .300 13 seasons, including 11 in a row, from 1921 to 1931.

Frank had a serious clash with McGraw and quit the club in 1926. After suspending Frisch, McGraw traded him to St. Louis for Rogers Hornsby, equally at odds with the Cardinals. The fiery Frisch had worn out his welcome with McGraw, but later admitted "I could have flopped as a ballplayer under any other teacher."

As second baseman and manager of the famous "Gashouse Gang," Frisch appeared in four World Series, winning one in 1931, and another in 1934, a year after becoming player-manager. Frisch won the first NL MVP Award in 1931, hitting .311 with 96 runs, 82 RBI, and a league-

FRISCH HAD A .319 CAREER AVERAGE.

leading 28 steals. Frankie's playing career ended in 1937, but he managed for 16 years, with St. Louis, Pittsburgh, and Chicago. He was elected to the Hall of Fame in 1947.

Lou Gehrig

On June 2, 1925, New York Yankees manager Miller Huggins inserted rookie first baseman Lou Gehrig as a late-inning defensive replacement. That day, Gehrig began a record streak of 2,130 consecutive appearances. Only rarely did he play just to extend his streak; Gehrig played because he was the best all-around first baseman ever.

Born in Manhattan, Henry Louis Gehrig (1903-1941) started his pro career in 1923. After two years in the minors, he moved to New York for good. In 1925, his first full major-league season, Gehrig hit .295 with 68 RBI. He never again scored or drove in under 100 runs in a full year.

In 1931, Lou established an AL record with 184 RBI, breaking his own mark of 175. He also once had three triples in a game that was rained out—in the fourth inning!

Gehrig's slugging exploits were only part of the story. He was also both an excellent baserunner and a solid first baseman. His two MVP Awards were given in recognition for Gehrig's contributions to a great Yankee team.

In 1934, Gehrig won the Triple Crown—his only batting title. Gehrig slumped badly in 1938 and early 1939. Lou benched himself on May 2, sitting out for the first time in nearly 14 years. Shortly afterward, tests revealed that he had amyo-

EMOTION OVERCOMES GEHRIG AS HE OFFICIALLY RETIRES FROM BASEBALL.

trophic lateral sclerosis—a terminal hardening of the spinal cord. Knowing he would soon die, Gehrig retired on July 4, 1939, at Yankee Stadium. Tearfully, he told the packed house, "Today, I consider myself the luckiest man on the face of the earth."

Charlie Gehringer

Never flamboyant, the almost Sphinx-like Charlie Gehringer might have gone virtually unnoticed on the baseball diamond but for his outstanding day-in, day-out performance. His unceasing excellence led to his nickname, "The Mechanical Man." Gehringer's manager Mickey Cochrane said of him, "He says hello on opening day and goodbye on closing day, and in between he hits .350."

Charles Leonard Gehringer (1903-1993) played both football and baseball at the University of Michigan and was given a tryout by none other than Detroit player-manager Ty Cobb.

Signed by the Tigers in 1924 as a third baseman, Gehringer soon moved to second base and became the club's regular second-sacker in 1926, where he remained for 16 years. After hitting .277 as a rookie, he batted over .300 nearly every season until 1941. As a defensive player, Gehringer led the AL in fielding percentage six times and paced the loop in assists seven times.

Gehringer's high-water mark came in 1937 when he rapped .371 to win the American League batting crown. Before that year, Gehringer also paced the junior loop on several occasions in runs, hits, doubles, triples, and stolen bases. His play in all departments was of such high caliber that he played in six All-Star games, hitting .500. He displayed the same steady brilliance in three World Series appearances with the Tigers. In 81 Fall Classic at-bats, Charlie hit .321, one point higher than his career average of .320.

CONSISTENCY AND AN EFFORTLESS STYLE MARKED GEHRINGER.

Gehringer retired at the end of the 1942 season with 2,839 hits and a .320 average and ended his career by leading the AL in pinch hits. Two years after he was elected to the Hall of Fame in 1949, Charlie returned to the Detroit Tigers as general manager.

Bob Gibson

In the 1960s, when power pitchers ruled the game, few were as dominant as Bob Gibson. Among the most successful of World Series performers, he set many records during his 17-year Hall of Fame career with the St. Louis Cardinals.

Robert Gibson (born 1935) overcame both the slums of Omaha and childhood illness to become an outstanding athlete. The Cardinals signed him in 1957, and he soon made the majors. However, poor control kept him from success until 1961, when Cardinals manager Johnny Keane put Gibson in the starting rotation.

Bob led the league in walks that year, but won 13 games. The following season he had 208 strikeouts,

the first of nine seasons of 200-plus Ks. In 1963, he was 18-9, and in 1964, his 19-12 record led the Cardinals to a world title. Gibson was intimidating in Series play, winning an NL-record seven games against two losses as the Cards took World Championships in 1964 and 1967, and lost in 1968.

IN 1968 BOB GIBSON PITCHED 13 SHUTOUTS AMONG HIS 22 WINS.

In 1968, Gibson won both the MVP and Cy Young Awards. His record was 22-9, with an NL-record 1.12 ERA and a league-best 268 strikeouts. In game one of the World Series that year, he had a single-game record 17 strikeouts.

Gibson was forced to stay in a private home during spring training in 1958, and the struggle to overcome racism stayed with him. He helped force the Cardinals' Florida hotels to accept blacks in the early 1960s.

Gibson won another Cy Young in 1970 with a 23-7 showing. He had over 20 wins in five seasons, and won in double figures 14 consecutive years. Gibson also smacked 24 lifetime home runs and won nine consecutive Gold Gloves.

Josh Gibson

Possibly the best known of the Negro League sluggers, Josh Gibson hit tape measure home runs that rattled off the seats and into history.

Joshua Gibson (1911-1946) was born in Buena Vista, Georgia, but grew up in Pittsburgh. An outstanding athlete, he won medals as a swimmer before turning to baseball. By age 16, he was a star for an all-black amateur team.

Josh, playing semipro ball by 1929, was watching a Homestead Grays game when their catcher broke his finger. The team pulled Gibson, already locally famous, out of the stands and into the game. Within two years, he was one of the team's biggest stars, hitting around 70 home runs a year. Lured to the Pittsburgh Crawfords in 1932, he caught Satchel Paige for five years.

Gibson was an unpolished catcher at first, but playing over 200 games a year (summer in the States and winter south of the border) helped Josh quickly become a fine backstop. Walter Johnson said Gibson was a better receiver than Hall-of-Famer Bill Dickey. Roy Campanella called Gibson "not only the greatest catcher but the greatest ballplayer I ever saw."

Gibson's drives in major-league parks reached unprecedented distances. He is credited with hitting a ball out of Yankee Stadium, and his longest hits are variously estimated between 575 and 700 feet. His home run total is uncertain, but even low estimates give him 800 to 950 career four-baggers. Gibson's lifetime average is the highest in Negro baseball, at .379 or .440, depending on the source. Against major-league pitching, he hit .424 with five homers in 16 exhibition contests.

Gibson went back to the Grays in 1936, and ultimately led them to nine straight Negro National League pennants. However, he began to drink heavily, partially in a search for relief from what was finally diagnosed a brain tumor. He died at age 35, one day after Jackie Robinson played his first game in the Dodger farm system. Gibson was named to the Hall of Fame in 1972.

Goose Goslin

Nicknamed Goose because of his last name and because of his large nose, Leon Allen Goslin (1900-1971) was originally a pitcher, but moved to the outfield when his first professional manager thought that Goose's bat had more promise than his arm.

While Goslin was leading the Sally League in hitting, Washington bought him for $6,000. Unfortunately, Goslin injured his arm while heaving a shotput early in 1922 and never again threw with his old ability. Mediocre defensively even before the injury, Goslin worked hard to become a competent outfielder.

Goose quickly emerged, though, as a standout slugger. In 1923 and 1925, he led the American League in triples. A year later he was the loop's RBI king. Even though he was a fine power hitter, Goslin could not rack up high home run totals while playing in Washington. The outfield fences in Griffith Stadium, his home park, were so distant that no Senator won a home run crown until the park was reconfigured in the 1950s. All 17 of Goslin's home runs in 1926 were hit on the road.

The Senators took AL pennants in 1924 and 1925 with Goslin's help. He won the 1928 AL batting crown, hitting .379, but in 1930 was dealt to the Browns. Washington owner Clark Griffith almost immediately regretted letting Goose go and worked to get him back.

Reobtained in December 1932, Goslin helped the

THE CLUTCH-HITTING GOSLIN HIT .344 IN THE 1924 WORLD SERIES.

Senators to win their third and last pennant the following summer. Griffith then swapped him to Detroit.

Goslin helped the Tigers win AL titles in 1934 and 1935, and produced the hit that won the 1935 World Series. Owner of a .316 lifetime average and 2,735 hits, Goose entered the Hall of Fame in 1968.

Rich Gossage

Rich led his league three times in saves, and registered 20 or more of them ten times in a career that spanned three decades.

Richard Michael "Goose" Gossage was born in 1951 in Colorado Springs. The White Sox drafted him in 1970, and brought him to the majors as a middle reliever two years later. Gossage was 7-1 in his debut season, and in 1975 paced the AL with 26 saves and registered a 1.84 ERA in 142 innings. He threw very hard and improved his control over the course of his career.

The next season, Goose started 29 games and completed 15 for the White Sox, but his 9-17 record brought an end to that experiment. He would never start another game in the majors. Gossage was dealt to the Pirates in 1977, and pitched in a career-high 72 games, finishing with an 11-9 record, 26 saves, and a remarkable 1.62 ERA in 133 innings.

The burly righthander signed with the Yankees as a free agent for the 1978 season, and over the next six years he collected 150 saves, twice pacing the AL. The relief role changed in the late 1970s, and managers began to use their closers less frequently. Gossage only once cleared the 100-inning mark after 1977, and this may have helped prolong his career.

He was the premier reliever of his day, and was voted to nine All-Star teams. Gossage also pitched in three AL playoff series while a Yankee. Only once in his six seasons in New York did his ERA clear 2.27, and that was in 1979, when it was just 2.62.

He joined the Padres in 1984, and his 10 wins and 25 saves helped San Diego to the NL championship. He registered 26 more saves and a 1.82 ERA in 1985, walking just 17 men in 79 innings. By the late 1980s, he was no longer used as a closer, but continued as a setup man into the 1990s.

Hank Greenberg

One of the many players to lose playing time to World War II, Hank Greenberg lost prime years. Active for only nine and one-half seasons, and serving in the Army for more than four, he still produced 331 career homers and a .313 average.

HANK GREENBERG TOTALED AN AMAZING 1,276 RBI IN 1,394 GAMES.

Bronx native Henry Benjamin Greenberg (1911-1986) was offered a contract by the Yankees in 1929. With Lou Gehrig at first base for the Yanks, Greenberg signed with the Tigers. In the Texas League in 1932, he hit 39 homers with 139 RBI. He was promoted to Detroit in 1933.

In 1934, Greenberg led the AL with 63 doubles and drove in 131 runs. In 1935, the Tigers won a World Championship, and Hank won the MVP Award, leading the league with 36 homers and 170 RBI. His 183 RBI in 1937 is the third highest total ever, and Greenberg's .92 career RBI per game is matched only by Gehrig in this century. Greenberg also clubbed 58 homers in 1938.

In 1940, he led the Tigers to another pennant, grabbing his second MVP Award and pacing the AL in doubles, homers, and of course, RBI. He also shifted from first base to left field to accommodate Rudy York. Unfortunately, Greenberg played only 19 games in 1941 before missing the next four seasons to World War II.

He returned in mid-1945 to lead the Tigers to the World Championship, cracking a pennant-winning grand slam on September 30. In 1946, he again led the AL in home runs and RBI.

A salary dispute sent Greenberg to Pittsburgh in 1947. He promptly retired, but Pittsburgh officials, desperate for his drawing power, met Greenberg's every demand. Hank played a final year before retiring, working extensively with young Ralph Kiner—another future Cooperstown inductee.

Lefty Grove

Many feel Lefty Grove is the greatest pitcher ever. He holds the highest career winning percentage of pitchers with 300 or more career victories, and Grove's 112-39 minor-league record gave him a combined winning percentage of .696, easily the best of any pitcher in organized baseball history.

Robert Moses Grove (1900-1975), a mine worker, decided at age 20 that baseball might offer a brighter future. Shortly after Grove joined the Blue Ridge League, Jack Dunn, owner of the Baltimore Orioles of the International League, purchased him.

For the next four and one-half years, Grove was unable to move up to the majors because Jack Dunn refused to sell him. Lefty was impatient to leave. Finally, in 1924, Connie Mack of Philadelphia paid Dunn $100,600 for Grove's contract.

Old control problems persisted during his first two seasons with the A's. In 1927, however, Grove improved his location dramatically and, not coincidentally, won 20 games.

The following year, Lefty led the AL in wins for the first of four occasions. In 1929, he paced the AL in winning percentage, a feat he repeated five times. That year, Grove also led the loop in strikeouts for the fifth of seven straight seasons. Nine separate times he topped the AL in ERA.

In 1930, he went 28-5, pacing the AL in winning percentage, ERA, and strikeouts, as the A's won the series over the Cards. Incredibly, his 1931 season was better. Lefty was 31-4, and his 2.06 ERA was over two runs below the league average! Grove received the first official AL MVP Award that year.

Traded to the Red Sox after the 1933 season, Grove collected four more ERA crowns. He retired in 1941 after winning his 300th game and was elected to the Hall of Fame in 1947.

Gabby Hartnett

Gabby Hartnett was the greatest catcher in the first 90 years of the National League. He talked a blue streak, handled pitchers well, and lasted for years on a good bat and a lot of savvy. Burleigh Grimes said that Gabby "had as good an arm as ever hung on a man."

Born in Woonsocket, Rhode Island, Charles Leo Hartnett (1900-1972) turned pro in 1921, batting .264 in the Eastern League. The Cubs bought his contract in 1922. When Hartnett took over in Chicago in 1924, he held the position until the late 1930s.

Gabby became a reliable stickman for several years, hitting in the .275 range with some power. After an arm injury in 1929, he exploded in 1930, hitting .339 with 37 homers and 122 RBI.

In 1935, Hartnett was the National League MVP. His .344 average was third in the league, and he led

CHARLES LEO HARTNETT LED THE CUBS ATTACK FOR 19 SEASONS.

NL catchers in assists, double plays, and fielding average as the Cubs won the pennant.

Hartnett left many career fielding records, but is best known for the "Homer in the Gloamin'" in a critical September 1938 contest. As player-manager of the Cubs, he led his team from nine games out in August to take the pennant from Pittsburgh. *The New York Times* reported, "In the thickening gloom, with the score tied and two out in the ninth inning...Hartnett blasted a home run before 34,465 cheering fans to give his Cubs a dramatic 6-to-5 victory over the Pirates." The Cubs won four pennants during Gabby's time with them: in 1929, 1932, 1935, and 1938. His last three years with the Cubs were as player-manager.

Red Smith wrote, "[Hartnett] was so good that he lasted 20 years in spite of the fact that he couldn't run. All other skills were refined in him."

Rickey Henderson

Rickey Henderson swiped Lou Brock's single-season and all-time stolen base titles, and in the process became acknowledged as the consummate leadoff hitter.

Rickey Henley Henderson (born on Christmas Day, 1957) was heavily recruited to play college football. Instead, he signed with his home-town Oakland Athletics. In the minors, he became the fourth player in professional baseball history to steal seven bases in one game. He was in Oakland's starting line-up by June 1979, and swiped 33 bases while hitting .274—and his production would only increase.

In 1980, Henderson became the third major-leaguer to steal 100 bases in a season. The next year brought Henderson's first Gold Glove, and league highs in hits, runs, and stolen bases. In 1982, Henderson smashed Brock's record of 118 pilfers in a single season with 130, and also led the AL in walks. He snatched 108 more bases in 1983.

Henderson topped the AL in stolen bases every season from 1980 to 1991, save for 1987, when he spent two months on the disabled list.

In December 1984, the Yankees gave Oakland five players to get Henderson. Despite injuries in 1985, Henderson finished his first Yankee season with 24 homers, 72 RBI, and 146 runs scored. The next season, he smashed 28 dingers, drove in 74, and scored 130. It was at this point that many began to regard Henderson as the best lead-off man ever.

The A's reacquired him in mid-1989 during a successful pennant run. In 1993, he helped Toronto win a World Series, then moved back to Oakland as a free agent. Henderson passed Brock in career swipes during 1991, and garnered his 1,000th steal in 1992. Combining on-base ability, speed, defense, and power, Rickey has been one of the most productive offensive players in modern baseball history.

Rogers Hornsby

With the exception of Ty Cobb, no superstar was more disliked than the aloof, independent, and caustic Rogers Hornsby. Modern authorities detract for his defense, but Hornsby was probably the greatest righthanded hitter ever. He led the NL in slugging percentage ten times and holds a .358 average.

Rogers Hornsby (1896-1963) began as a shortstop in the Texas-Oklahoma League. In 1915, the Cardinals bought his contract.

Hornsby hit .313 as a rookie. In 1917, his second full season, he topped the National League in slugging and was second in batting. He also led all league shortstops in double plays.

Hornsby slipped below the .300 mark for the only

HORNSBY IS CONSIDERED ONE OF THE BEST-EVER SECOND BASEMEN.

time in his major-league career in 1918, but ranked high in all slugging departments. Moved to third base in 1919, "The Rajah" again finished second in batting average. The following spring, Hornsby shifted to second base, led the NL in RBI, and hit a league-best .370.

No one expected Rogers to duplicate that figure in 1921. Instead, he upped the ante to .397 and then batted

.401 in 1922, .384 in 1923, .424 in 1924 (a 20th century NL record), and .403 in 1925 to make him the only player to average over .400 for a five-year span. He also won the triple crown in 1925. In 1926, Hornsby was made player-manager and promptly led the Cardinals to their first world title that season.

A dispute with St. Louis owner Sam Breadon resulted in a trade to the Giants before the 1927 season. The cantankerous Hornsby moved from the Giants to the Braves to the Cubs in three years, but led the league in slugging percentage each year. Hampered by injuries, Hornsby quit as a full-time player after the 1931 season and was voted into the Hall of Fame in 1942.

Carl Hubbell

Carl Hubbell, "The Meal Ticket," won 253 games and lost 154 while posting a remarkable 2.97 earned run average in his 16-year career with the New York Giants.

Carl Owen Hubbell (1903-1988) grew up in Oklahoma. He started pitching for an oil company team after high school, finally turning pro in 1923. Hubbell threw a baffling screwball, which broke toward lefty batters, unlike a curve, which broke away from lefty batters. Carl was sold to the Tigers in 1925, who nixed the screwball, fearing it would ruin his arm. His performance was inferior, and he was optioned to the minors.

After two mediocre seasons, Hubbell was released from Detroit in 1928 and began pitching in the Texas League. Giants scout Dick Kinsella discovered Hubbell, and Giants skipper John McGraw paid $30,000 for him.

Hubbell tossed the NL's only no-hitter in 1929, but his big years didn't really begin until 1933. He registered five straight 20-win seasons starting that season. King Carl also pitched an 18-inning shutout against the Cardinals, won two games in the World Series without allowing an earned run, and was voted the league's Most Valuable Player.

The following season, he had his most famous moment. In the second All-Star Game, Hubbell fanned Babe Ruth, Lou Gehrig, Jimmie Foxx, Al Simmons, and Joe Cronin in succession.

Hubbell won the MVP again in 1936 when he turned in one of the best pitching records in history at 26-6. Hubbell had finished 1936 with 16 straight wins, and won his first eight in 1937, for a 24-game winning streak. Elbow damage from throwing his screwball necessitated surgery after the 1938 season, and Hubbell was never the same. However, his peak was so strong that the Hall of Fame elected him in 1947.

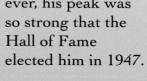

Joe Jackson

Some fans prefer to remember sweet-swinging "Shoeless Joe" Jackson as one of the greatest outfielders of all time. Others simply recall that he was one of eight men banned from baseball for throwing the 1919 World Series.

Joseph Jefferson Jackson (1887-1951) signed with Philadelphia, but the largely uneducated Jackson felt uncomfortable with big-city life and was soon released. He fared better in Cleveland, where he stayed until early 1915, when he was sold to the White Sox.

For a four-year stretch, Jackson averaged better than .390. In 1911 he batted .408, and the next season hit .395, but finished second to Ty Cobb both times. Joe compiled a tremendous .356 lifetime average, third only to only Ty Cobb and Rogers Hornsby.

The 1919 AL champion White Sox were favored to beat the Reds in the World Series, but lost five games to three. Accusations flourished concerning the performances of several Sox players. During the 1920

SHOELESS JOE JACKSON NEVER HIT BELOW .300 IN A FULL SEASON.

season, eight players, including Jackson, were charged with accepting bribes to throw the Series. The accused players were banned from baseball for life.

Jackson, who batted .356 in 1920, his final season, maintained his innocence until his death. In the 1919 Series, he topped all players with a .375 average, but committed two costly errors in the field.

After being banned, Jackson returned to South Carolina. He played for semipro teams under assumed names and lived comfortably. His supporters have made continuous but unsuccessful attempts to convince the baseball establishment that Jackson belongs in the Hall of Fame.

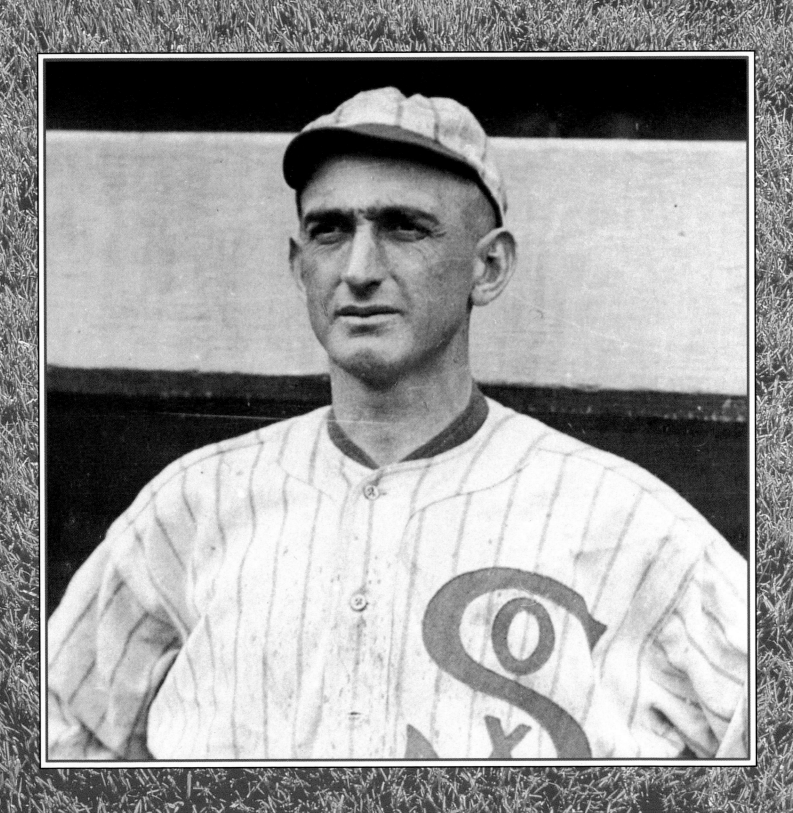

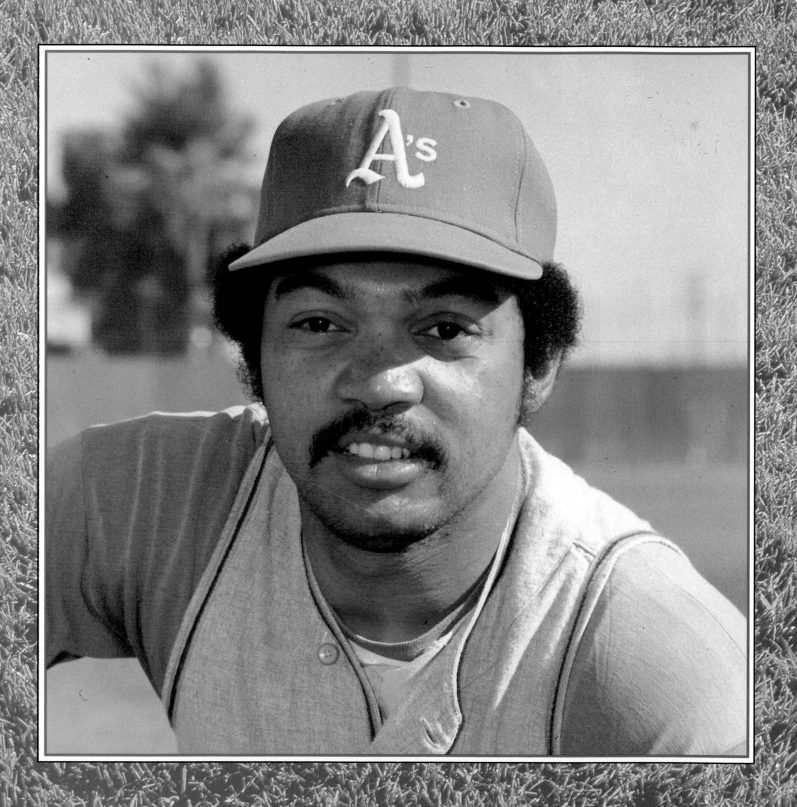

Reggie Jackson

Reginald Martinez Jackson was born in 1946 in Wyncote, Pennsylvania. His father, Martinez, a Negro League player, passed on athletic talent and a sturdy upbringing. Reggie's athleticism and outspoken nature attracted scrutiny, but his ability transcended the hype and led Jackson to the Hall of Fame.

Jackson, an outstanding high school athlete, went to Arizona State as a defensive back and a baseball player, and became the second player picked in the 1966 draft by Kansas City. Debuting in 1967 with the A's, he blossomed as the franchise moved to Oakland in 1968, hitting 29 homers with 74 RBI. Reggie became a superstar in 1969, leading the league with 123 runs and a .608 slugging percentage.

In 1971, Jackson hit 32 homers as Oakland won the first of five straight Western Division titles. He matched his 32-homer output in 1973, when he won the AL MVP. The years from 1972 to 1974 brought three straight World Series Championships.

Free agency broke up the A's, and Jackson was traded to Baltimore in 1976. A year later, he joined the Yankees, where he clashed with manager Billy Martin and owner George Steinbrenner. Jackson called himself "The Straw that Stirs the Drink," alienating himself from teammembers. But in game six of the 1977 World Series, Jackson hit three homers to deliver the title to the Yanks; he became "Mr. October."

After five years in New York, Jackson moved to the California Angels, helping them to first-place finishes

TEN WORLD SERIES HOMERS EARNED JACKSON THE NAME "MR. OCTOBER."

in 1982 and 1986. A graceful and athletic outfielder as well as a world-class hitter, Jackson captured four AL home-run crowns and finished with 563 homers in 21 big-league seasons.

Ferguson Jenkins

Ferguson Jenkins never walked more than 83 hitters in a season. He won 20 games for the Cubs each season from 1968 to 1972 on his way to 284 career wins, and he is the only pitcher in baseball history to fan more than 3,000 batters while walking fewer than 1,000.

A graceful, durable 6'5" right-hander from Chatham, Ontario, Canada, Ferguson Arthur Jenkins (born 1943) labored in the Philadelphia organization for three-plus years before a promotion in 1965. The Phillies used Fergie as a reliever, but Chicago obtained him in 1966. Cubs manager Leo Durocher made Jenkins into a starter late that season. In 1967, he was 20-13 with a 2.80 ERA for the Cubs. It was the

JENKINS WON THE CY YOUNG IN 1970.

first of six consecutive 20-win seasons. He led the National League with 40 starts in 1968, and went 20-15, losing a record five 1-0 decisions.

Jenkins's best Cub season was 1971, when his league-leading 325 innings pitched and 24 wins won him the Cy Young Award. He was 20-12 in '72, but slipped to 14-16 in 1973, and the Cubs sent Jenkins to Texas for Bill Madlock.

In 1974, he led the American League with a career-high 25 wins and fanned 225. In '75, he was 17-18 with a 3.93 ERA. Boston traded three players for him that winter, and, despite injury, he was 12-11. After a run-in with Red Sox manager Don Zimmer, Fergie was shipped back to Texas. He won 46 games over the next three years, and ended his career with the 1983 Cubs.

Jenkins led the league in strikeouts in 1969 and fanned more than 200 six times. Like other control pitchers, he allowed many homers; his 484 round-trippers allowed are the second-most ever. In 1991, Jenkins was elected to the Hall of Fame by one of the closest margins in Cooperstown history.

Walter Johnson

Nicknamed "The Big Train" by sportswriter Grantland Rice, Walter Johnson won 416 games in 21 years with the Washington Senators. No other pitcher in this century has won so many. In addition, no other pitcher could have won nearly as many games with the teams for which Johnson played.

When he joined the Nats in 1907, they had yet to finish higher than sixth place or have a pitcher who won 20 games in a season. Walter Perry Johnson (1887-1946) soon remedied the latter shortcoming, but even his talents couldn't immediately lift the team out of the nether regions. The Senators finished last or next to last in each of Walter's first five seasons, even though he twice won 25 games. Then in 1912, Washington vaulted to second place as Johnson racked up 32 wins, 303 strikeouts, and a 1.39 ERA. When Walter suspended belief the following year, winning 36 games and posting a microscopic 1.09 ERA, the Senators repeated their second-place finish. Eleven more years passed before Washington again returned to contention.

Those who wrote Walter off, though, were in for a surprise. In 1924, with Washington locked in a season-long pennant fight, Johnson paced the AL in winning percentage, strikeouts, and ERA. His league-leading 23 wins also helped bring the Senators their first flag. In the World Series, Johnson won the deciding seventh game in relief. The following season he spurred Washington to a second consecutive pennant when he again won 20. The Pirates, however, bested him in game seven of the series.

The Big Train retired as a player after the 1927 season. His 2.17 career ERA is the seventh-best total ever, and Johnson is the only pre-1960s pitcher in the top ten all-time strikeout leaders. Johnson was among the first five players elected to the Hall of Fame in 1936.

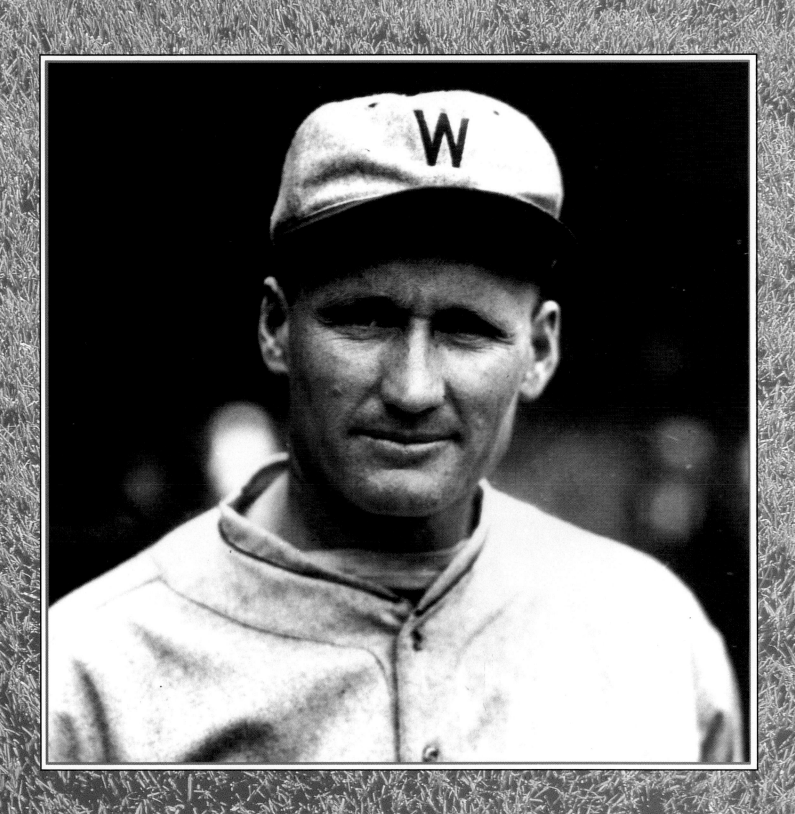

Judy Johnson

Of the Negro Leaguers recognized by the Hall of Fame, Judy Johnson has perhaps the weakest batting stats. His fielding at third base is usually described as steady or intelligent rather than spectacular. Yet most who played with him or saw him agreed that he was a great player.

William Julius Johnson was born October 20, 1900, in Snow Hill, Maryland. He got his break in 1918 when World War I called many black players away from baseball.

He joined the powerhouse Philadelphia Hilldales in 1921, taking over the third base job. A line-drive hitter, he drove in a high number of runs despite not hitting many homers.

Johnson played with Philadelphia for 11 years (from 1921 to '29 and 1931 to '32). He hit a career-high .406 in 1929, a year in black baseball that matched white baseball in 1930 for high offensive totals. Sportswriter Rollo Wilson chose him MVP for the season. Judy moved to the Homestead Grays as a player-manager the next year.

Johnson was a member of perhaps the best Negro League team in history when he joined the Pittsburgh Crawfords in 1932. The well-heeled Crawfords raided the Pittsburgh-based Homestead Grays and other teams for the best black players money could

buy. With the Crawfords, Johnson played alongside immortals such as Satchel Paige, Josh Gibson, and Cool Papa Bell. Johnson finished his playing career with the Crawfords in 1938.

Later, Johnson became a fine major-league scout, when organized baseball began to accept blacks. "I could have gotten Hank Aaron [for the Athletics] for $3,500," said Judy. "I got my boss out of bed and told him I had a good prospect and he wouldn't cost too much, and he cussed me out for waking him up at one o' clock in the morning." He later landed Dick Allen for the Phillies and spent many years teaching young players the fine points of pro ball. The Hall of Fame enshrined Johnson in 1975.

Al Kaline

There is a storybook quality to the career of Al Kaline, who joined the Detroit Tigers as an 18-year-old boy and retired a 40-year-old Hall of Fame legend. He hit for average and power, and played near-perfect defense with a rocket arm. He is among the brightest—and best loved—in a galaxy of Detroit stars.

Albert William Kaline (born 1934) was raised to be a baseball player; his grandfather, father, and uncles played semipro ball. After hitting .488 as a Baltimore high school senior, Kaline signed with the Tigers for $30,000. Al saw his first big-league action as a pinch-hitter the day he signed out of high school.

In Kaline's second full season, 1955, he became the youngest player ever to win a batting title, hitting .340 with a league-best 200 hits and 27 home runs. He finished a close second in the MVP vote to Yogi Berra. Al batted .314 in 1956 with 27 homers and a career-high 128 RBI.

As good as Kaline was, and teammates like Norm Cash, Jim Bunning, and Rocky Colavito were, the Tigers were a mediocre team for most of Al's career. From 1957 to 1967, Al pulled his weight, batting between .280 and .300, with 18 to 25 homers and 70 to 100 RBI despite a congenital foot injury.

The Tigers jelled in 1968, winning the pennant, but Kaline broke his leg and

AN ALL-AROUND PERFORMER, AL KALINE NEVER PLAYED IN THE MINORS.

played in only 102 games. He recovered by the World Series and batted .379 with eight RBI as the Tigers won their first World Championship since 1945. Kaline collected his 3,000th hit in his final season, 1974, and was a first-ballot Hall-of-Famer in 1980.

Tim Keefe

Tim Keefe, like most 19th century 300-game winners, played with good teams for much of his career. The durable hurler labored 4,103 innings and collected 285 victories in his first nine full seasons. He posted only a 57-51 record in his last five seasons, but his 342 wins are the eighth-highest total in history.

Massachusetts native Timothy John Keefe (1857-1933) played only amateur ball until age 22. After a season with Utica in the National Association, he was signed by Troy of the National League in 1880. Troy already had an outstanding rookie pitcher in Mickey Welch, but early in the 1881 season, however, Keefe began to prove himself the more tireless worker and won the top job on the staff.

When the Troy franchise moved to New York in 1883, Keefe joined the New York Metropolitans of the rival American Association. After the team won the 1884 pennant, Keefe and several teammates were moved to the National League entry in New York, which was renamed the Giants. The shift was easy, albeit somewhat unethical, since both Gotham clubs boasted the same ownership.

Reunited in 1885, Keefe and Welch helped the Giants win National League pennants in 1888 and 1889. After the 1889 season, however, Keefe and many teammates joined the Brotherhood's revolt and jumped to the New York franchise in the Players League.

The New York club was expected to win in 1890, but finished third as arm trouble held Keefe to 17 victories. Returning to the National League, Keefe pitched three undistinguished seasons, then retired to become an umpire. He was named to the Hall of Fame in 1964.

TIM KEEFE'S 1887 CARD AS A MEM-BER OF THE NEW YORK GIANTS.

Harmon Killebrew

The top righthanded home-run hitter in AL history, Hall-of-Famer Harmon Killebrew had over 40 home runs eight times and over 100 RBI in ten seasons. He won six AL homer crowns and slugged 573 career homers in 22 years.

Born in 1936, Harmon Clayton Killebrew was an All-State quarterback in Idaho. At 17, he was recommended to the Senators by Idaho Senator Herman Walker, who wanted to see his young constituent in the majors. Killebrew blasted a 435-foot homer for scout Ossie Bluege, who signed "Killer" immediately.

He was a third baseman when he came up, and though he eventually played more games at first than third, he had significant playing time at the hot corner until 1971. He eventually earned outstanding AL left fielder, third baseman, and first baseman honors from *The Sporting News*.

Killebrew, a bonus baby, didn't play full-time until 1959. He was ready for the role, leading the league with 42 home runs. He hit 31 the next year, after which the Senators became the Minnesota Twins. Harmon hit 46 for his adoring new fans in 1961, but that year Roger Maris hit 15 more. Killebrew led the league in 1962, 1963, and 1964, hitting 142 longballs in the three seasons, and driving in 333 runs.

Killebrew won the AL MVP Award in 1969 with 49 homers, 140 RBI, and 145 walks, leading the league with a .430 on-base percentage. He paced the league four times in walks. Through criticized for low batting averages, his on-base totals were among the best in the league.

ONLY BABE RUTH HIT MORE AL HOMERS THAN KILLEBREW.

Harmon's 90 homers in in 1969 and 1970 helped the Twins win two AL West division titles. Age and knee problems slowed Harmon in the 1970s, and he retired after the 1975 season.

Ralph Kiner

The greatest slugger in the years immediately following World War II, Ralph Kiner won a National League record seven-straight home run titles. Only Babe Ruth has a career home-run ratio better than Kiner's.

Ralph McPherran Kiner (born 1922) was a renowned semipro player in Alhambra, California. After high school graduation in 1940, he signed with Pittsburgh. He played in the minors for two and one-half seasons before joining the Navy in mid-1943.

After his release in December 1945, Ralph said, "I got myself into just sensational shape. Sure enough, I had a spring training like no one's ever had." In 1946, Kiner became the Pirates' left fielder, and his 23 home runs led the league.

In 1947, Pittsburgh acquired Hank Greenberg, and the Pirates shortened the left field fence from 365 feet to 335 feet (an area known as "Greenberg's Garden"). Ralph hit 51 homers in 1947, with guidance from Greenberg.

Hank retired after 1947, and left field became "Kiner's Korner." Ralph slugged 40 homers in 1948 and 54 in 1949. Though Forbes Field helped Kiner, he twice set road home run records. He walked 100 or more times six-straight years, posting an excellent lifetime on-base average of .397. Kiner scored over 100 runs in six seasons. Despite the poor quality of Pirate teams during his career, Kiner was recognized as one of the game's great stars.

Kiner was a hard and innovative worker. "I obtained a filmstrip of Babe Ruth's swing, broken down frame-by-frame, which I copied carefully and practiced whenever I got the chance." He had films taken of his own swing to spot flaws, and took extra batting practice. He was a four-time *Sporting News* All-Star and a prime mover in the player's movement, which led to the pension plan and the financial bonanza for modern players. Later, Ralph became a popular broadcaster for the New York Mets.

Sandy Koufax

Over a five-year span, lefthander Sandy Koufax led the NL in ERA five times and compiled a 111-34 record before arthritis forced him to retire at age 30.

Koufax, born in Brooklyn in 1935, signed with his hometown Dodgers in 1954. He started only five games in 1955, alternately brilliant and completely wild. The Dodgers moved to Los

KOUFAX THREW 11 SHUTOUTS IN '63, A MODERN RECORD FOR LEFTIES.

Angeles before the 1958 season, and Koufax was 27-30 over the next three years. He threw hard with excellent movement, but had not yet learned how to pitch.

Early in 1961, catcher Norm Sherry urged Koufax to slow down and throw changeups and curveballs. Following that advice, Sandy went 18-13 and led the league with an eye-popping 269 Ks. In 1962, the Dodgers moved to Dodger Stadium and Koufax was 14-7 with a no-hitter and a league-leading 2.54 ERA, though he missed time with a finger ailment.

A healthy Koufax returned in 1963. He went 25-5, leading the NL with a 1.88 ERA, 11 shutouts, and 306 strikeouts. He won

both the MVP and Cy Young Awards, tossed another no-hitter, and won two games in the World Series. In 1964, he was 19-5 with a league-best 1.74 ERA, but was shelved by a deteriorating arthritic condition in his arm. He pitched in 1965 and 1966, aided by cortisone shots and ice, and won two more Cy Young Awards. He collected 26 and 27 wins and league-best ERAs of 2.04 and 1.73. Koufax also tossed two more no-hitters, including a perfect game.

The Dodgers won NL crowns in 1963, 1965, and 1966, mainly due to his brilliance. One of the best pitchers ever while at his peak, Koufax has kept a low profile since being voted into the Hall of Fame in 1972.

Nap Lajoie

In 1896, Napoleon Lajoie (1874-1959) was purchased by the Philadelphia Phillies from the minors. By 1901, the Phils were pennant contenders. A salary hassle with owner Colonel Rogers, however, induced Lajoie to jump to the Philadelphia Athletics of the fledgling American League when A's manager Connie Mack offered a lucrative four-year pact.

Lajoie set a 20th century record by batting .422 and winning the AL Triple Crown in 1901. The smarting Phillies, however, obtained a court injunction that prohibited Lajoie from playing with any other team in Philadelphia. Since the injunction applied only in Pennsylvania, Mack traded Lajoie to Cleveland for whom he could play anywhere but Philly. Due to the legal wrangling, Lajoie got into only 87 games in 1902, but rebounded to lead the AL in hits in 1903 and 1904.

In all, Lajoie won three American League batting crowns, though his 1910 title is still disputed. Nap edged Ty Cobb by a single point after getting eight hits in a season-ending double-header, six of them bunts that Lajoie beat out as St. Louis Browns third base-man Red Corriden played deep to deny the hated Cobb the title.

Few of Lajoie's other accomplishments are taint-ed, however. For the first 13 years of the 20th century, he was the AL's Honus Wagner—the greatest field-er at his position of his time and also a great offensive player. Just the third man to collect 3,000 hits, Lajoie's lifetime average is .338.

Unlike Wagner, who played on four pennant win-ners in Pittsburgh, Lajoie was never on a champ. Lajoie, who spent time as Cleveland's player-manager, was so pop-ular that the team was renamed the "Naps" in his honor. Although Lajoie stepped down as manager following the 1909 season, he remained with Cleveland five more seasons. He concluded his career with the A's and was elected to the Hall of Fame in 1936.

Buck Leonard

Buck Leonard, a power-hitting first baseman, often drew comparisons to Lou Gehrig. Buck, one of the Negro Leaguers in baseball's Hall of Fame, was a key part of the dominating Homestead Grays of the 1930s.

Walter Fenner Leonard (born 1907) was born in Rocky Mount, North Carolina. He played semi-pro baseball until 1933, when the Depression forced him to pursue baseball as a primary occupation. Leonard was signed by the Baltimore Stars. Buck traveled with the team until it disbanded. Stuck in New York, he signed with the Brooklyn Royal Giants. Leonard then stopped in a New York bar owned by Joe Williams, a retired Homestead Grays

player who had his eye open for talent; the Grays had been all but wiped out by player raids and retirement.

Leonard signed to play first base for the Grays. The team began to regain respectability, and when Josh Gibson came aboard in 1937, the Grays caught fire, winning nine consecutive flags. When Gibson jumped ship to play in Mexico in 1940, Leonard carried the club, hitting .392 in 1941 to lead the Negro National League. He won another batting title when he was 39 years old, at .395, and a pair of home-run titles in his long career.

The Homestead Grays split their home games between Pittsburgh and

Washington. Since they filled both stadiums, they paid their stars more than other Negro League teams. The lure of Mexican baseball was also a boon to Leonard; the Grays were forced to match the salary he was offered to play south of the border, and he commanded over $1,000 per month in 1942. He stayed with the Grays for his entire career, instead of jumping to other teams as many players did.

Buck did play winter ball in Mexico, Cuba, Puerto Rico, and Venezuela, and barnstormed with Satchel Paige's all-stars. Leonard closed out his storied career with a .312 average for Durango of the Mexican Leagues at the tender age of 48 and was named to the Hall of Fame in 1972.

Pop Lloyd

Pop Lloyd jumped from semipro baseball to the black professional leagues in 1905 at age 21, and was good enough to play semipro until age 58. A fine defensive shortstop during his early years, he also showcased a line-drive stroke that drove his average to dizzying heights.

John Henry Lloyd (1884-1964) started in semipro ball as a teenager. Pop, like other gifted players of his generation, began his career as a catcher, but by 1907, he was a shortstop and a cleanup hitter with the Cuban X-Giants. Lloyd performed for various Philadelphia teams, New York and New Jersey teams, and with the Chicago American Giants, among others. Lloyd was in demand for barnstorming tours, but the uncertain finances of the black leagues often forced him to miss spring training to work a conventional job.

In a 1910 12-game exhibition series in Cuba against Detroit, Lloyd went 11-for-22. While the Bengals won seven of 12 games, Ty Cobb was sufficiently embarrassed to vow never to play against blacks again. In 1914, Pop joined the American Giants and teamed with "Home Run" Johnson to help Chicago win championships in 1914 and 1917.

Lloyd was often likened to Honus Wagner, a comparison Wagner was proud to acknowledge. Like Honus, Lloyd was a terrific hitter, and was known to scoop up dirt along with ground balls. In Cuba, Pop was "El Cuchara," Spanish for "The Shovel."

LLOYD WAS REGARDED AS THE BEST SHORTSTOP OF HIS DAY.

At age 44 in 1928, Pop hit .564 in 37 games, with 11 homers and ten steals. The next year, he hit .388. Not only was Pop a great hitter, but he had an intimate knowledge of the game, spending several years as a player-manager in the Negro Leagues. Lloyd was named to the Hall of Fame in 1977.

Mickey Mantle

Mickey Mantle was the most feared hitter on the most successful team in history, and overcame great pain in his storied career.

Mickey Charles Mantle was born in 1931 in Spavinaw, Oklahoma. A standout school player, he beat osteomyelitis, a condition that at one time nearly cost him his left leg.

The Yankees signed Mickey, originally a shortstop, in 1949. The next year, he led the Western Association with a .383 batting average, 141 runs, 199 hits, and 55 errors.

Mickey opened the 1951 season in right field with the Yankees, but was soon sent to the minors. Mickey's dad persuaded him not to give up, and he soon returned.

Mantle eventually took over in center field for Joe DiMaggio in 1952. "The Commerce Comet" led the Yanks to seven World Championships and owns records for homers, RBI,

MANTLE'S 18 HOME RUNS IN WORLD SERIES PLAY ARE THE MOST EVER.

runs, walks, and strikeouts in Series play. He won his first of four homer titles in 1955.

In 1956, Mantle won a Triple Crown with 52 homers, 130 RBI, and a .353 average. He also captured the first of three MVP Awards. He won again in 1957, hitting .365 with 34 homers, 94 RBI, 121 runs, and 146 walks.

Mantle notched homer crowns in 1958 and 1960, then dueled with Roger Maris to break Ruth's record in 1961. While Maris won with 61, Mick hit 54, and led the AL with a .687 slugging percentage, 132 runs scored, and 126 walks. Mick again won an MVP in 1962.

Mantle's many injuries shortened his career. After two painful seasons in 1967 and 1968, The Mick retired with 536 home runs. Mantle was inducted to Cooperstown in 1974.

Rabbit Maranville

Walter James Vincent Maranville (1891-1954) was nicknamed "Rabbit" by fans who were captivated by the way the diminutive shortstop hopped about the infield. At 155 pounds, Maranville is the smallest 20th century player in the Hall of Fame. Maranville posted only a .258 career batting average and a .318 on-base percentage. It was for his peerless glove and strong leadership that Maranville earned his reputation.

Maranville was purchased from the minors in 1912 by the Boston Braves. During spring training in 1913, Maranville won the shortstop job with hustle and good defense.

A poor team for over a decade, the Braves took the

MARANVILLE HOLDS THE ML RECORD FOR MOST PUTOUTS BY A SHORTSTOP.

1914 National League pennant after being in last place as late as July 4. Manager George Stallings was nicknamed "The Miracle Worker" for the team's stunning triumph and second baseman Johnny Evers won the MVP Award, but some feel Maranville was the real catalyst of the Braves' surge.

Rabbit, known for zany off-the-field antics, once dove fully clothed into a

hotel fountain and reportedly surfaced with a goldfish clenched between his teeth. Traded to Pittsburgh following the 1920 season, he had his finest year as a hitter in 1922, batting .295 and scoring 115 runs.

Maranville began slipping in the field, though, and was sent to the Cubs in 1925. Appointed player-manager in July, he was released after only eight weeks. Idled most of 1926 by an injury, he was banished to the minors by St. Louis in 1927. The pink slip so shocked Rabbit that he stopped drinking and began working harder, and by the end of the season he had been recalled.

Maranville remained a stellar defensive shortstop until 1934 when his career was ended by a broken leg.

Juan Marichal

Juan Marichal won more games, 191, than any pitcher during the 1960s. He was a good strikeout pitcher, but also the greatest control artist of his time, walking just 709 men in over 3,500 innings. His delivery defied logic. The timing oddities and whirl of motion that resulted from his high-kick windup baffled hitters for 16 seasons.

Dominican-native Juan Antonio Marichal y Sanchez (born in 1937) signed with the Giants in 1958 and led the Midwest League with 21 wins and a 1.87 ERA. Marichal paced the Eastern League in '59 with 18 wins and a 2.39 ERA, and was 11-5 the next year in the Pacific Coast League.

Called to San Francisco in mid-1960, Marichal went 6-2 with a 2.66 ERA. In 1963, Marichal led the NL with 25 wins and pitched a no-hitter. He also bested Warren Spahn in a 16-inning complete game win. 1963 was the first of six 20-win seasons in seven years for "Manito," and each season his ERA was under 3.00.

On August 22, 1965, Marichal batted against Sandy Koufax. Juan had thrown a few brushbacks, and when Dodger receiver John Roseboro asked Koufax to retaliate, Sandy refused. Marichal, thinking Roseboro's throws to Koufax ticked his ear, slugged the catcher several times with his bat. A vicious fight ensued. Marichal was suspended and fined, and since the Giants finished just two games back of the flag-winning Dodgers, his absence was costly.

The incident may have kept Marichal, who was 243-142 lifetime, from ever winning a Cy Young Award, and he did not make the Hall of Fame until 1983. Perhaps the best righthander of the 1960s, he finished in the top three in wins five times and ERA three times. He feasted on the Dodgers, beating them in 37 of 55 decisions. Ironically, he spent 1975, his last season, with Los Angeles. "The Dominican Dandy" compiled a lifetime 2.89 ERA.

Eddie Mathews

Eddie Mathews teamed with Hank Aaron to form a lethal one-two punch in the 1950s and early 1960s. Mathews, who hit 512 career homers, was the best-hitting third baseman in history before Mike Schmidt.

Edwin Lee Mathews (born 1931) was pursued by the Brooklyn Dodgers, who offered a $10,000 contract. He was also courted by the Boston Braves, who offered $6,000. Eddie decided that Boston would give him the best opportunity. Mathews batted .363 with 17 homers in 1949, his first pro season, and slugged 32 homers the next year in the Southern League.

Mathews was promoted to Boston in 1952, and though he led the NL in strikeouts, he cracked 25 homers. The next year, the Braves left for Milwaukee and Mathews's 47 round-trippers led the NL. He notched 37 or more taters and 95 or more RBI from 1954 to '56. In 1957, he batted .292 with 32 homers and 94 RBI as the Braves won a World Championship.

He hit just .251 with 31 four-baggers as the Braves won another pennant in 1958, but Eddie won the homer crown in 1959 with 46. Mathews hit at least 30 homers in nine seasons, a National League record, and four times hit over 40. He led the league in walks four times and scored at least 95 runs in ten straight seasons. While Henry Aaron and Mathews played together, they hit 863 home runs, more than Babe Ruth and Lou Gehrig. Mathews was elected to baseball's Hall of Fame in 1978.

Mathews, initially a poor defensive player, eventually became a capable third baseman. He led the NL in putouts twice and assists three times. He is sixth among third sackers in career double plays.

In 1962, Mathews injured his shoulder, and his ability gradually declined. After one year in Atlanta in 1966, he was traded to Houston and later to Detroit before retiring in 1968.

Christy Mathewson

Christy Mathewson signed his first baseball contract in 1899. Seventeen years later, he retired with 373 victories and universal recognition as the greatest pitcher in National League history to that time.

Christopher Mathewson (1880-1925) probably did more than any contemporary to enhance the image of a professional baseball player. Educated, intelligent, and a consummate gentleman, he seemed almost too good to be true.

Mathewson, originally Giants property, was drafted by Cincinnati for $100 in 1900, after a short trial with New York. John Brush, part-owner of the Reds who was planning a move to the Giants, clandestinely returned Matty to New York for aging Amos Rusie.

Beginning in 1903, Mathewson reeled off 12 straight seasons of 20 or more victories. "Big Six" won over 30 games on four occasions, capturing 37 in 1908. He had 300 career victories by age 32.

Sometimes, Mathewson struggled in the "big games." In his last three World Series appearances—1911, 1912, and 1913—Matty won just two games while losing five. In his defense, the Giants scored only seven runs in the last 39 innings he hurled in Series play.

However, Mathewson did some fine work in championship contests. In 1905, his first World Series, he tossed a record three complete-game shutouts against the Philadelphia Athletics to lead the Giants to victory in their first 20th century postseason affair. Matty's feat may be the greatest performance in Series history.

In 1916, with his famed "fadeaway" screwball no longer effective, Mathewson was traded to Cincinnati to become the Reds player-manager. He entered the Army in August 1918. While serving overseas, Matty accidentally inhaled poison gas, permanently damaging his lungs and leading to death from tuberculosis in 1925. His 2.13 ERA is fifth-best in history. In 1936, Christy was one of the initial five players elected to the Hall of Fame.

Willie Mays

Few players had the total package of Hall-of-Famer Willie Mays. He was a beautiful fielder with a strong arm, a powerful and consistent hitter, a canny base-runner, and a durable champion.

Born in 1931 in Westfield, Alabama, Willie Howard Mays joined the Birmingham Black Barons in 1947. The Giants signed him in 1950, and Mays batted .353 in the Inter-State League.

In 1951, the Giants promoted Willie, who became Rookie of the Year. Hitting 20 homers and playing an excellent center field, he galvanized the Giants, who came from 13½ games back to win the NL title. Mays won the hearts of teammates and fans with his enthusiasm, humor, and, above all, his stellar performances.

An Army stint in 1952 and 1953 robbed Mays of the chance to break Babe Ruth's all-time homer title. (Willie finished with 660.) In 1954, Willie won the MVP Award, pacing the NL in batting average and slugging percentage. His remarkable catch of Vic Wertz's drive in that year's World Series is one of baseball's greatest moments.

Willie led the NL with 51 homers in 1955, and hit over 35 homers 11 times. He totaled 40 homers six times, twice topped 50, and won five slugging crowns. In addition to his power, average, arm, and defense, he won four stolen base and three triples titles.

"THE SAY HEY KID"

In 1962, Mays hit 49 homers and the Giants again won the NL crown. In 1964, he won his second MVP, batting .303 with 35 home runs and 111 RBI. The next year, he hit .317 with 52 round-trippers and 112 RBI.

Mays won a dozen Gold Gloves in a row and retired with records for games, putouts, and chances for center fielders. The lifetime .302 hitter ended his career in the 1973 World Series.

B*ill* M*azeroski*

The 1960 World Series between the Yankees and the Pirates was one of the most unusual series ever. The Bronx Bombers won games by scores of 16-3, 10-0, and 12-0 and outscored the Pirates 55-27. But the Bucs won the tourney when, in bottom of the ninth inning of a tied game seven, Bill Mazeroski's homer off Ralph Terry gave the Pirates a dramatic 10-9 triumph.

William Stanley Mazeroski (born 1936) played all of his 17 big-league seasons with Pittsburgh, beginning in midseason in 1956. He received his first All-Star invitation in 1958, hitting .275 with 19 homers, and leading NL second sackers in assists and chances.

In 1960, Mazeroski led the league in five defensive categories, including a sterling .989 fielding percentage. He also hit .273 with 11 homers and 64 RBI. Maz batted .320 with two round-trippers and a team-leading five RBI in that famous World Series.

MAZEROSKI'S 2,094 GAMES AT SEC-
OND BASE ARE A CLUB RECORD.

In 1966, he had 16 four-baggers and a career-best 82 RBI. Forbes Field, his home park, masked his power; Maz hit 93 of his 138 round-trippers on the road.

Mazeroski won eight Gold Gloves. Injuries led to an early decline for Mazeroski, and he retired after the 1972 season. He still holds several major-league records for second sackers, including most double plays in a single season (161 in 1966), most career double plays (1,706), most seasons with the league lead in assists (nine), and most seasons leading the league in double plays (eight). His double-play pivot was especially famed. He also finished his career with 2,016 hits and 853 RBI. The Pirates retired his No. 9 in 1987.

Willie McCovey

The "other" Willie on the 1960s San Francisco Giants was one of the great sluggers of the decade, averaging 30 homers a year and leading the league in round-trippers three times.

Willie Lee McCovey (born 1938) was signed by the Giants in 1955, and promptly led the Georgia

MCCOVEY WON THE NATIONAL LEAGUE MVP AWARD IN 1969.

State League with 113 RBI. In 1958, Willie hit .319 with 89 RBI in the Pacific Coast League. Unfortunately,

the Giants had 1958 Rookie of the Year Orlando Cepeda at first base. After "Stretch" hit .372 with 29 homers in 95 PCL games in 1959, he went to San Francisco and belted 13 homers with a .354 average in 52 games to himself become Rookie of the Year.

In 1960, however, McCovey slumped and returned to the minors. In 1961 and 1962 he hit 38 four-baggers in half-time play before winning an everyday job in 1963. He promptly led the league with 44 home runs, but slumped due to injuries in 1964.

The Giants reached the World Series in 1962. In the ninth inning of the seventh game, McCovey, with the tying and winning runs

on, lined out—"the hardest ball I ever hit"—straight to second base.

McCovey won the National League MVP Award in 1969, pacing the loop with 45 homers and 126 RBI. He led the circuit in slugging percentage in 1967, 1968, and 1969. After a .289 average and 39 homers in 1970, he missed much of the next two years with various ailments.

The popular but aging and injury-prone McCovey was traded to the Padres in 1974. In 1977, he returned to the Giants, and batted .280 with 28 homers to win the National League Comeback Player of the Year Award. He is tied with Ted Williams with 521 career home runs. McCovey was named to the Hall of Fame in 1986.

Johnny Mize

Hard-hitting first baseman Johnny Mize, who led the NL in homers four times, linked the great 1930s Cardinal teams to the Yankee dynasty of the 1950s.

John Robert Mize (1913-1993) of Demorest, Georgia, signed with Greensboro of the Piedmont League while still in high school. In 1933, while in the International League, Mize was purchased by the St. Louis Cardinals.

Mize joined the Cards in 1936 and batted .329 with 19 home runs. He developed his power and also hit .300 for the next eight seasons, peaking at .364 in 1937. In 1939, Johnny led the league in homers and batting average. In 1940, "The Big Cat's" 43 dingers topped the NL, and his 137 RBI also led the league. Mize paced the NL in slugging percentage annually between 1938–40. He hit .312 lifetime, and walked around 75 times a season.

Traded to the New York Giants, Mize led the NL in 1942 with a .521 slugging percentage and 110 RBI. He served three years in

MIZE PLACED IN THE TOP THREE IN OFFENSIVE CATEGORIES 54 TIMES.

the Navy, but returned in 1946 to top the NL twice more in home runs. His 51 round-trippers in 1947 are still an NL lefty record. Mize also paced the loop in RBI and runs scored.

Late in the 1949 pennant drive, the Yankees acquired him for $40,000. After pounding 25 homers in just 274 at bats in 1950, Mize was the hero of the 1952 World Series. He hit .400 with three homers, grabbing Series MVP honors. Johnny led the AL in pinch hits from 1951 to '53.

The Big Cat won five World Series rings with the powerful Yanks. He retired after the 1953 season. The only slugger in history to hit three home runs in a game six times, Mize was named to the Hall of Fame in 1981.

Joe Morgan

Hall-of-Famer Joe Morgan is best remembered as the catalyst for the World Champion Reds in 1975 and 1976. He also played more games at second base than anyone but Eddie Collins.

Joe Leonard Morgan, born in 1943, grew up in Oakland. His first hero was Jackie Robinson, but later Morgan emulated Nellie Fox, who would one day coach him. Joe signed with the Astros in 1963. In 1964, he was the Texas League MVP, batting .319 with 42 doubles, 12 homers, and 90 RBI.

In 1965, Morgan won the Houston second base job. The 5'7" Morgan hit .271 with 14 home runs, 100 runs scored, and a league-leading 97 walks to finish second in Rookie of the Year voting. He scored 94 runs in 1969, 102 in 1970, and 87 in 1971. Before the 1972 season, the Astros dealt Morgan to Cincinnati in one of the biggest trades of the 1970s.

Joe's fame grew when he left the Astrodome. He hit 16 homers in 1972, 26 in 1973, and 22 in 1974. He walked 346 times and scored 345 runs those three years. He also won Gold Gloves from 1973 to 1977.

In 1975-76, Morgan became the only second sacker to win back-to-back

MVP Awards. He batted .327 in 1975 with 17 homers, 94 RBI, 67 stolen bases, and a league-best 132 walks. Morgan then hit .320 with 27 dingers in 1976.

JOE MORGAN HIT MORE HOMERS THAN ANY OTHER SECOND BASEMAN.

Joe returned to Houston and led the Astros to the NLCS in 1980. In 1983, he hit 16 homers for the NL-champion Phillies. He hit .271 lifetime with 268 home runs and 689 steals, and is third all-time for walks.

Eddie Murray

Strong, dependable Eddie Murray averaged 28 homers each of his 12 seasons as a Baltimore Oriole, and drove in at least 78 runs every year.

Standards of excellence were set early for Eddie Clarence Murray (born 1956), who played high school baseball in Los Angeles with future major-leaguers Ozzie Smith and Darrell Jackson.

A third-round pick by the Orioles in 1973, Murray made three minor-league All-Star teams. A natural right-hander, he taught himself to switch-hit. In 1977 at age 21, he broke into the big leagues with style, becoming the fourth Oriole to capture AL Rookie of the Year honors. Murray was also the first major-league player to win the trophy while appearing mostly as a designated hitter.

Placed at first base in 1978, Murray continued his excellent production at bat while thriving in the field. He won three straight Gold Gloves, from 1982 to '84, and was among the best at

MURRAY'S SWITCH-HITTING STATS ARE SECOND ONLY TO MICKEY MANTLE'S

fielding bunts and gaining force-outs at second base.

Murray continued to improve at bat, and in 1983 posted then-career highs in home runs, runs, and walks. Eddie led the Orioles to a resounding victory over the Phillies in the 1983 World Series.

Except for the 1981 strike year, he had at least 84 RBI per season each of his 12 Oriole campaigns. He continued to produce after his days in Baltimore, hitting .330 with the 1991 Dodgers and smacking 27 homers for the 1993 Mets.

Murray's involvement in community work led to nominations for the Roberto Clemente Humanitarian Award in 1984 and '85 for sponsoring medical, educational, and religious foundations.

Stan Musial

Stan "The Man" Musial starred with the St. Louis Cardinals for 22 seasons and was the first National League player to win three Most Valuable Player Awards.

Stanley Frank Musial was born in 1920 in Donora, Pennsylvania. Signed as a pitcher in 1940, he also played the outfield. He injured his pitching shoulder that year, and moved to left field full-time. Musial was in the majors by the end of 1941.

In 1942, the Cardinals won the World Series as rookie Musial hit .315. In 1943, Stan won his first MVP Award with an NL-best .357 average, 220 hits, 48 doubles, and 20 triples.

Musial had good power, was terrifically fast, and played excellent defense, both in left field and later at first base. He won six slugging titles, and his unique corkscrew batting stance led to seven batting crowns. Musial posted a lifetime .331 batting average and scored 100-plus runs 11 straight times.

Stan won his second MVP in 1946 as the Cards took another World Championship. He led the league with a .365 batting average and 50 doubles. He won his third MVP trophy in 1948, missing the Triple Crown by a single homer. His .376 average was the NL's highest since in 1930, and his 230 hits, 46 doubles, 18 triples, and 131 RBI led the league.

Stan won batting crowns from 1950 to 1952 and took his final batting title in 1957 at age 37. He collected his 3,000th hit a year later.

MUSIAL RECEIVES A GOLDEN BAT FOR WINNING THE BATTING TITLE IN 1952.

Musial hit .330 in 1962, when he was 42, and was named the 1946-55 "Player of the Decade." "The Donora Greyhound" was voted into baseball's Hall of Fame in 1969.

164

Kid Nichols

When he first joined the Boston Beaneaters in 1890, Charlie Augustus Nichols looked so youthful and unprepossessing that he was called "Kid." The nickname stuck with him for the remainder his of his 14-year big-league career, during which he won 361 games (including 273 during the 1890s, more than any other pitcher of the decade), sixth-best on the all-time list.

Nichols (1869-1953) began his career in 1887 with his hometown Kansas City club in the Western League. After two seasons, Nichols landed with Omaha in the Western Association. Frank Selee, Omaha's manager, was hired to skipper the Boston Beaneaters the next year and brought Nichols with him.

Kid Nichols is the only 300-game winner in major league history who got by with just a fastball (and a none-too-overpowering fastball at that). What Nichols had in spades was control. When he walked a batter, it was usually because he preferred not to let him hit.

He won 30 or more games eight times for Boston, reaching a high of 35 in 1892. Five years he pitched over 400 innings, and over 300 in 11. Never a strikeout or ERA leader, Kid nevertheless topped the National League three times in shutouts and always ranked among the leaders in complete games and saves (staff aces were also used in relief back then).

The 1890s Beaneaters were baseball's best team, largely due to Nichols. However, team owner Arthur Soden lost several of his stars in the early 1900s when he refused to match offers made to them by new American League clubs. Nichols quit the Beaneaters and bought a share of the Kansas City team in the Western League.

After two years as a player-manager with Kansas City, Kid was lured back to the majors by the St. Louis Cardinals, who offered him the same dual role. He won 21 games for St. Louis in 1904 and finished his career with the Phillies two years later. At age 36, Nichols had tossed over 5,000 innings in 582 games. Nichols was named to the Hall of Fame in 1949.

Mel Ott

Mel Ott stood out even in an era of great sluggers for his youth, his odd batting stance, and his great performance over nearly two decades.

Melvin Thomas Ott (1909-1958) of Gretna, Louisiana, was a three-sport high school star. He played semipro ball at age 16 for a team with connections to John McGraw.

McGraw himself eventually gave Ott a tryout. Impressed with his hitting ability, even though Mel had an odd batting technique, McGraw signed Ott but refused to send him to the minors, fearing a farm skipper would alter Ott's stance and "ruin" him.

Ott's stance was certainly unique. He lifted his front foot before swinging, his hands held almost below his belt. The result was a level swing with terrific power, amply announced by 42 home runs and 152 RBI in 1929, his second full year.

OTT SPENT HIS ENTIRE 22-YEAR CAREER WITH THE NEW YORK GIANTS.

He also led the league in 1929 with 113 walks, a sign of the discipline that would lead to a lifetime on-base average of .410. He was just 20, and his youthful appearance and size (5'7", 160 pounds) reinforced the impression of youth that stayed with him throughout his career. In fact, Ott made the Hall of Fame when he was just 42.

Ott was a fine outfielder with a great arm, leading NL outfielders in double plays in 1929 and 1935. Ott benefited greatly from his home park, hitting just 187 of his 511 homers on the road. Mel was a World Series hero in 1933, hitting .389 with two homers, one winning the final game in the tenth inning.

Mel became player-manager of the Giants in 1942 but failed to win a pennant. Known for his sweet disposition, he was also a taskmaster as a manager, and helped the careers of such players as Johnny Mize. A 1958 car crash took Ott from this world too soon.

Satchel Paige

Sometimes Satchel Paige seems more myth than flesh-and-blood. He was the most popular baseball player in the Negro Leagues, and was still baseball's biggest draw after integration. He pitched into his sixties, and few who faced him could help but acknowledge his greatness.

Leroy Robert Paige (1906-1982) was born in Mobile, Alabama. His birthday is recorded as July 7, 1906. He was signed by the semipro Mobile Tigers in 1924, and from 1927 to '30 he was with the Birmingham Black Barons. Paige joined the Pittsburgh Crawfords in the 1930s. Paige also pitched in the Caribbean.

Paige had two amazing fastballs: "Long Tommy" was supersonic, and "Little Tommy" was merely unhittable. He also threw his "bee ball," which would "be where I want it to be."

When Paige barnstormed, fans insisted he pitch every day. He regularly got the best of top major leaguers; Joe DiMaggio said Satchel was "the best I ever faced."

Overuse led to a sore arm in 1939. In response, Satchel developed several off-speed pitches and a baffling hesitation delivery. When his arm recovered in 1940, he was even better than before.

Finally, in 1948, Indians owner Bill Veeck gave Paige a chance and the 42-year-old legend was signed. Paige was 6-1 with a 2.47 ERA over 73 innings, and pitched before packed houses as Cleveland won the World Series.

Paige's 123 recorded Negro League wins, 179 big-league appearances, and Hall of Fame plaque

EVER INSIGHTFUL, SATCHEL TRIES TO IMPART HIS PITCHING SAVVY UPON KANSAS CITY HURLERS.

only hint at his greatness. A colorful speaker, his six rules for "How to Stay Young" became famous, the sixth being "Don't look back. Something might be gaining on you."

Jim Palmer

The image of Jim Palmer as a sex symbol and TV pitchman diminishes his accomplishments as one of the game's top right-handed hurlers. Palmer won 20 games in eight seasons, won 15 games a dozen times, and compiled sub-3.00 ERAs ten times.

James Alvin Palmer (born 1945) spent just one year in the minors before the Orioles promoted him in 1965. In 1966, he was inserted into the starting rotation and went 15-10 for the pennant-winning Birds. Jim gained fame that fall at age 20 by shutting out the Dodgers in game two of the World Series, defeating Sandy Koufax in the final game of his career.

Palmer missed most of the next two years with an arm injury, but came back in 1969 to win 16 games and pace the AL in winning percentage. In 1970, he began a streak of four consecutive 20-win seasons. In 1973, he won his first Cy Young Award with a 22-9 record and a league-best 2.40 ERA. After elbow problems in 1974, he rebounded to become one of the top hurlers in baseball. He led the AL in 1975 with a 2.09 ERA and 23 victories to cop his second Cy Young. He paced the AL in victories in 1976 (earning another Cy Young) and 1977, and won 20 in 1978.

Palmer allowed his share of home runs, but in 3,984 innings, never gave up a grand slam. Despite various injuries, he led the league in innings pitched four times. With Palmer on the staff, the Orioles won the American League West from 1969 to '71, 1973 to '74, and 1979.

Jim and Oriole manager Earl Weaver were both highly competitive men. The two had many run-ins, but their relationship was not as rocky as many believed. Palmer retired in 1984 with a 2.86 career ERA, 268 wins, and 2,212 Ks. Over his 20-year career with the Orioles, Palmer compiled many club pitching records, and also picked up four Gold Gloves. He was named to the Hall of Fame in 1990.

Gaylord Perry

Gaylord Perry—the only pitcher in history to have won the Cy Young Award in both leagues—fooled hitters and umpires for 22 years. An admitted proponent of the spitball, he entitled his autobiography *The Spitter and Me*. He maintained that simply the idea of using a spitball put hitters at a disadvantage.

Gaylord Jackson Perry, born in Williamston, North Carolina, in 1938, is the younger brother of fellow major-league hurler Jim. Gaylord was first called to San Francisco in 1962. He became a regular starter in 1964, and responded well, with a 2.75 ERA. In 1966, he posted a 21-8 mark and a 2.99 ERA. He kept his ERA under 3.00 for four straight years, tossed a no-hitter in 1968, and led the NL with 23 wins in 1970.

Traded to the Indians for a used-up Sam McDowell before the 1972 season, Perry won the AL Cy

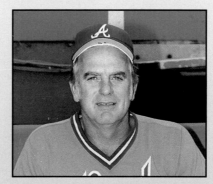

SPITBALL OR NOT, PERRY'S PITCHES UNNERVED MAJOR-LEAGUE BATTERS.

Young Award with a 24-16 mark and a 1.92 ERA. He was 19-19 in 1973, and the next year brother Jim joined him in Cleveland. In '74, Jim was 17-12 and Gaylord went 21-13. Their 38 victories represented half of Cleveland's 1974 win total.

Although Gaylord won 70 games for Cleveland in just over three years, he was traded to Texas. Three years later, he returned to the NL, and won the 1978 Cy Young Award with a 21-6 season for the Padres. He won his 300th game for Seattle in 1982, and ended his career with Kansas City in 1983 using a rosin-coated "puff ball."

Perry won 314 games with a remarkable 3.10 ERA. His 3,534 strikeouts rank him No. 6 on the all-time list, and his 5,351 innings pitched are in the lifetime top ten. Perry retired after the 1983 season and was elected to the Hall of Fame in 1991.

Eddie Plank

Before enrolling at Gettysburg College, Eddie Plank had no organized baseball experience. He was age 21 at the time and had spent his entire life on a farm. However, Gettysburg coach Frank Foreman, a former major-league pitcher, cajoled Plank into trying out for the varsity. From unlikely beginnings came a Hall-of-Fame career.

THE DELIBERATE PLANK THREW EIGHT SHUTOUTS IN 1907.

Although nearly 26 when he graduated in 1901, Edward Stewart Plank (1875-1926) was signed by the Philadelphia A's of the fledgling American League. Plank became a bane not only of enemy hitters, but also of umpires and sportswriters. His pitches were straightforward, but Plank worked so deliberately that he seemed to take forever between deliveries. Plank's quiet demeanor and lack of overpowering stuff made him poor newspaper copy.

He won 20 or more games in a season seven times for the A's, a club record he shares with Lefty Grove. Plank never led the American League in wins, ERA, or strikeouts, nor was he ever considered the A's staff ace. He became one of the few Hall of Famers to ride the bench for an entire World Series when Mack instead used Jack Coombs and Chief Bender in the 1910 classic.

After slipping to 15 wins in 1914 and losing the second game of the World Series that fall, Plank deserted the A's to play in the renegade Federal League. Thus, his 300th win came in the uniform of the 1915 St. Louis Terriers.

The following year, the St. Louis Browns signed Plank. He finished his career in 1917 as the first southpaw in major league history to win 300 games. Plank still holds the record for the most wins and the most shutouts by an AL lefthander.

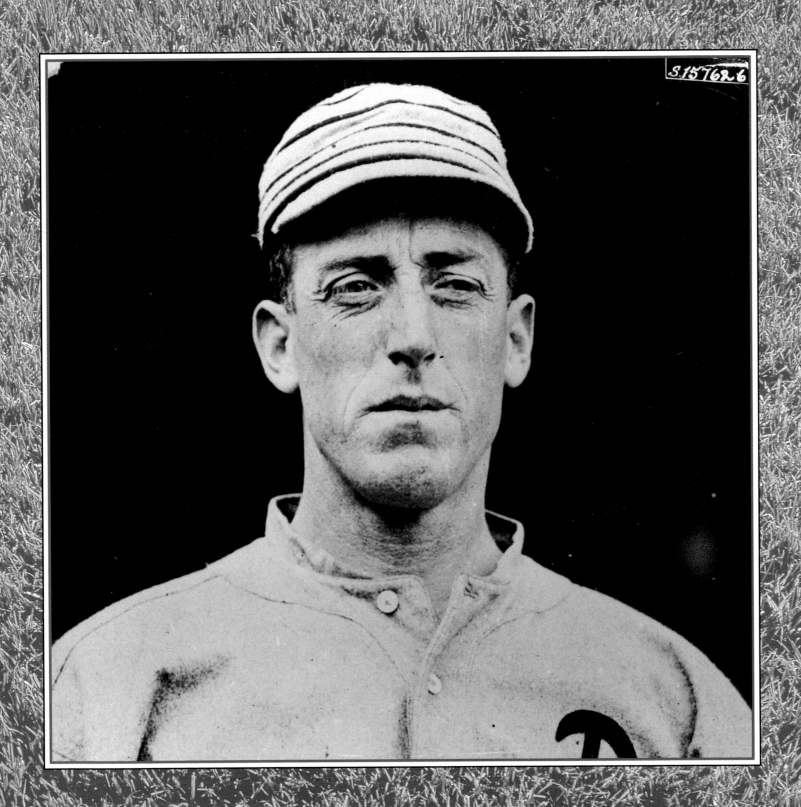
S.157626

Pee Wee Reese

Shortstop Pee Wee Reese was the leader of the 1940s and 1950s Brooklyn Dodgers. He was a fine defensive player and helped the Bums win seven National League titles. In 1984, the Hall of Fame inducted him.

Harold Henry Reese was born in Louisville in 1918. Pee Wee was signed by Louisville of the American Association in 1938, and spent two solid seasons there. The Red Sox owned the rights to Reese, but Branch Rickey of the Dodgers spent $75,000 to obtain him in 1940.

While Reese wasn't a great player immediately, he became important to the Dodger club. After three years in the Navy, he returned to the Dodgers in 1946 and began to increase his average, steal bases, draw walks, and hit for power. He scored 132 runs in 1949 to pace the NL, led the circuit in walks in 1947, and clubbed as many as 16 home runs in a season. Reese also stole 232 career bases and posted on-base percentages over .370 eight times. He was voted to ten straight All-Star teams and finished in the top ten in MVP voting eight times.

Pee Wee also had solid defensive skills. After committing 47 errors in his rookie year of 1941, Reese improved and became arguably the finest NL defensive shortstop of his time. He led the NL in fielding percentage just once, but had excellent range.

Reese's teammates were lavish in their praise of him. Though, like some team-

REESE ATTEMPTS TO LEG OUT A DRIVE AGAINST THE PIRATES.

mates, he requested a trade when Jackie Robinson was signed, Reese soon changed his mind. Pee Wee then befriended Jackie, and other disgruntled Dodgers soon fell in line. Robinson and the other pioneering black Dodgers have repeatedly cited Pee Wee for helping them on their difficult road.

Cal Ripken Jr.

Cal Ripken had a job to do, and he did it every day. His consecutive-game streak makes Cal the only player with a record of durability close to that of the revered Lou Gehrig.

While many modern players are derided for not putting enough effort into

RIPKEN LED THE ORIOLES TO A WORLD CHAMPIONSHIP IN 1983.

their jobs, Ripken never sat. His streak began in 1982, and he played 8,243 straight innings before sitting out the last two frames of a

September 1987 blowout. He had played 1,897 straight games through the 1993 campaign.

Drafted by the Orioles in 1978, Calvin Edwin Ripken Jr. (born 1960) made his pro debut that year in the Appalachian League. He was an Oriole by late 1981.

In 1982, his first full big-league season, he clubbed 29 home runs and chalked up 93 RBI to become the American League Rookie of the Year. After starting at third base, he shifted to shortstop in mid-season. At 6'4", Cal is the tallest full-time shortstop in major-league history.

In 1983, Ripken was the AL's Most Valuable Player, and led Baltimore to a World Championship. He

hit .318 with 27 homers and paced the loop in hits and doubles.

The next year, Ripken batted .304 and again smacked 27 home runs. Ripken led the league in assists, putouts, double plays, fielding percentage, and chances per game at various points in his career, and has collected two Gold Gloves. His brother, Billy, was the Orioles' regular second baseman for several years, and his father, Cal Sr., managed the team during the late 1980s.

After several productive, but unspectacular, campaigns, Ripken exploded in 1991. He hit .323 with 34 homers and 114 RBI to win his second MVP Award and re-establish himself as one of the AL's top all-around players.

Robin Roberts

Robin Roberts won 20 or more games each season from 1950 to 1955. He pitched in the majors for 19 years, and won 286 games.

Robin Evan Roberts (born 1926) was raised in Springfield, Illinois. He attended Michigan State University on a basketball scholarship in 1945, but eventually found his way to the diamond. He tossed two no-hitters at MSU and was signed by the Phillies in 1948.

The lanky righthander joined the Phillies later in 1948 and went 7-9. Philadelphia finished sixth in '48, third in '49, and won the NL title in 1950.

In 1950, Roberts went 20-11 and was among the league leaders in nearly every significant category.

That year was the first of six consecutive 20-plus win seasons for Roberts, but it was his only shot at a championship.

Roberts compiled a 28-7 mark in 1952, leading the league by a ten-win margin.

CONTROL ARTIST ROBIN ROBERTS WAS A SEVEN-TIME ALL-STAR.

He also paced the NL in victories from 1953 to 1955. Robin led the league in games started six straight years and complete games from 1952 to '56. He also won strikeout crowns in 1953 and 1954. He had outstanding control and extraordinary durability, leading the NL in innings four straight times while allowing very few walks. His great control also led to an all-time record of 505 home runs allowed, but the lack of enemy baserunners kept Roberts's ERAs low. Four times, he held opposing hitters to the lowest on-base percentage in the league.

The poor quality of his teams did not dim his ardor for baseball. His career ERA in 4,689 innings was 3.41. In addition to being a Hall-of-Fame pitcher, Roberts was also a key player in the development of the Players' Association.

Brooks Robinson

Brooks Robinson revolutionized the third base position. He did with reflexes and intelligence what can't be accomplished with just quickness and a strong arm. He won 16 Gold Gloves and started 15 straight All-Star games. Upon his retirement, Robinson held almost every major fielding record for third basemen, including games (2,870), fielding average (.971), putouts (2,697), assists (6,205), and double plays (618).

Born in Little Rock, Arkansas, in 1937, Brooks Calbert Robinson was signed by Baltimore in 1955, and by 1960 was the regular Oriole third baseman. For the next four years, he was a respectable offensive and defensive performer.

In 1964, Robinson's .317 average, career-high 28 homers, league-leading 118 RBI, and sterling glove work earned him AL MVP honors even though the Orioles finished third. Frank Robinson joined Baltimore in 1966, and the Birds won their first World Series. Brooks contributed a .269 average, 23 homers, and 100 RBI.

Robinson's work in the 1970 World Series earned him MVP honors; he hit .429 with two home runs and a highlight reel full of defensive gems. "The Human Vacuum Cleaner" dominated the Series as perhaps no other defender ever has.

In 23 seasons, Brooks had over 20 homers six times, and cleared 80 RBI eight times. He collected 2,848 hits, 268 home runs, and 1,357 RBI. Robinson led AL third basemen in assists eight times, fielding average 11 times, putouts and double plays three

BROOKS ROBINSON MAKES ONE OF MANY SENSATIONAL STOPS AT THIRD.

times, and total chances per game twice. After retiring in 1977, he became a popular broadcaster in Baltimore. Robinson's 1983 induction into the Hall of Fame drew one of the largest crowds ever seen at Cooperstown.

Frank Robinson

Frank Robinson was the first player to win Most Valuable Player Awards in both leagues and the first African-American manager in the majors.

Born in 1935, Frank Robinson signed with Cincinnati in 1953. He led the Sally League in 1954 with 112 runs scored, batting .336 with 25 homers and 110 RBI.

Robinson joined the Reds in 1956 and won the Rookie of the Year Award, leading the league with 122 runs and hitting .290 with 38 homers. His excellent production from 1957 to '60 made him one of the top outfielders in the National League.

Robby was also a fine defensive player with good speed, and won a Gold Glove in 1958.

Frank's 1961 MVP performance led the Reds to a pennant. He paced the loop with a .611 slugging percentage and batted .323 with 37 homers, 117 runs scored, 124 RBI, and 22 stolen bases. The next year, he led the NL in slugging percentage for the third consecutive time.

In December 1965, he was dealt to Baltimore. Cincinnati GM Bill DeWitt said, "Robinson is not a young 30." All the supposedly finished Robinson did in 1966 was win the Triple Crown and MVP Award, hitting .316 with 49 homers. He also smacked

two home runs as the O's won the World Series. The Orioles won AL pennants from 1969 to '71; Robinson hit 85 homers in that span.

In 1974, Robinson went to Cleveland, and the next year was named the Indians' player-manager.

IN 1961 ROBINSON PACED THE NL IN RUNS SCORED FOR THE REDS.

Only Babe Ruth, Willie Mays, and Hank Aaron socked more home runs than Frank's 586. In 1982, the Hall of Fame opened its doors to Robinson.

Jackie Robinson

For much of our country's history, a color line excluding African-Americans extended everywhere. A great inertia needed to be overcome to create the equality promised by our Constitution. That first high-profile integration came on a baseball diamond, and the first black man to cross the white lines was Jackie Robinson.

Jack Roosevelt Robinson (1919-1972) starred in four

ROBINSON'S TEN-YEAR CAREER WITH BROOKLYN HELPED ALL OF BASEBALL.

sports at UCLA and attracted the attention of Brooklyn Dodger GM Branch Rickey. After an Army stint, Robinson joined the Negro Leagues' Kansas City Monarchs. Rickey sought out and signed Robinson expressly to break baseball's color barrier. Aside from his outstanding baseball skills, Jackie possessed a strong and unbending character. From the beginning, Jackie was everything Rickey wanted.

Robinson broke in with Montreal of the International League in 1946. In 1947, Robinson was Rookie of the Year playing first base for Brooklyn. He later recalled his lowest day of that year being his first visit

to Philadelphia, where "hate poured forth from the Phillies dugout." Jackie said he was never closer to quitting.

Robinson didn't quit, though. Instead, he took the next step, winning a batting title in 1949 at .342 and capturing the MVP Award. Though he played just ten seasons, he helped the Dodgers to six World Series. The most devastating baserunner of his day, he also had dangerous power and fanned only 291 times in over 5,000 plate appearances. He became the first African-American elected to the Hall of Fame in 1962.

Pete Rose

Pete Rose is baseball's all-time leader with 4,256 career hits. In 1985, he garnered his 4,193rd safety to break Ty Cobb's record. Still, Rose is not in the Hall of Fame.

Rose, like Cobb, squeezed every bit of production from his talent. Both men seemed slightly out of place off the diamond, and both had gambling troubles at the end of their careers. Cobb was exonerated, but, acting on evidence that suggested Rose had bet on baseball games while managing the Reds, Commissioner Bart Giamatti banned Rose from baseball for life in 1989.

The Reds signed 140-pound Cincinnatian Peter Edward Rose (born 1941) in 1960. He spent the off-season pumping iron, and led in runs, hits, and triples his next two years in the minors.

Rose debuted in 1963 as Cincy's second sacker, and his enthusiasm endeared him to hometown fans. Taking a walk, he dashed to

"CHARLEY HUSTLE" RAPS ONE OF HIS MAJOR-LEAGUE RECORD 4,256 HITS.

first emulating Enos Slaughter; Whitey Ford dubbed Rose "Charley Hustle." Rose's .273 batting average and 101 runs scored won him the Rookie of the Year Award.

Rose came back in 1965 to lead the NL in hits and putouts. He was named to his first of 17 All-Star teams. In 1967 the Reds moved Rose to the outfield, and in 1968 and '69 he captured batting titles.

Rose led the "Big Red Machine" to four World Series between 1970 and '76. In 1973, he batted .338 and won the NL MVP. He amassed a 44-game hitting streak in 1977, and collected hit #3,000 the next year.

Rose signed with Philadelphia and played on the 1980 World Championship squad. He finished his career as a player-manager with the Reds in 1986, compiling a .303 lifetime average.

Amos Rusie

Amos Rusie is one of the few players in the Hall of Fame who spent fewer than ten seasons in the major leagues. Despite losing over two years due to disputes with his employers, Rusie won 245 games and paced the NL in strikeouts five times.

Born in Mooresville, Indiana, Amos Wilson Rusie (1871-1942) was signed at age 18 by the Indianapolis Hoosiers (then in the National League), who valued the local boy for his drawing card appeal and blinding velocity.

By 1890, Rusie had joined the New York Giants, and led all National League hurlers with 341 strikeouts. Gotham was not an ideal milieu for the young fireballer, however, who soon developed a drinking problem to go along with his control problems on the mound. Worse, he could not escape miserly Giants owner Andrew Freedman, one of the most repressive owners in major league history.

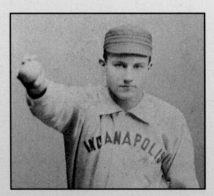

AMOS RUSIE LED THE NATIONAL LEAGUE IN ERA TWICE.

In the pitcher's box, though, "The Hoosier Thunderbolt" was in his element. Rusie's blazing speed helped convince the game's rulemakers to move the pitching mound from 50′ from home plate to 60′6″.

After topping the loop in whiffs again the next three seasons, Rusie held out in 1896 when Freedman attempted to fine him and cut his pay. Returning in 1897, when the other clubs kicked in $5,000 to reimburse him for his lost 1896 salary, Rusie had two more strong years with the Giants. Wounded again by Freedman's skinflint methods, he sat out 1899, then missed the 1900 campaign while he tended to his ill wife.

Rusie tried to return in 1901, but his arm was gone. The overpowering hurler was named to the Hall of Fame in 1977.

Babe Ruth

When he entered the majors in 1914, Babe Ruth was a pitcher. In fact, he was a great pitcher, with a 94-46 lifetime record. His bat, however, convinced the Red Sox to make him an outfielder in 1918. Ruth led the league with 11 home runs. The finest baseball player ever was flexing his muscles.

In 1919, George Herman Ruth (1895-1948) set a new mark with 29 home runs. However, Boston owner Harry Frazee's financial needs prompted Ruth's sale to the New York Yankees. "The Sultan of Swat" brought $100,000, over twice the price of any previous player.

Ruth took New York, baseball, and America by storm in 1920. His 54 home runs were more than any other AL team hit. His .847 slugging percentage is still a single-season record, and he batted .322 with a league-leading 158 runs and 137 RBI. He led the AL in home runs 12 times, runs scored eight, and RBI six. He paced the AL in slugging percentage 13 times. His 60 four-baggers in 1927 and 714 career home runs stood as records for well over 30 years. The Babe led the Yankees to four World Championships, helping to initiate a popular new high-offense baseball that helped

heal the wounds left by the 1919 Black Sox scandal.

He might have won more honors, but was suspended in 1922 for barnstorming, and played only 98 games in 1925 due to an intestinal abscess. The Bambino led the league in walks 11 times, drawing a record 170 in 1923. He was a fast runner, became a fine outfielder, and could have been an immortal pitcher.

Beyond his on-field heroics, Ruth—one of the first five Hall of Fame inductees in 1936—was a legend for his off-the-field adventures as well. His appetite for life led him to every excess. He ate everything, drank everything, tried everything, and made friends everywhere. Ruth was the most beloved man ever to play the game.

Nolan Ryan

The single-season and all-time strikeout leader, Nolan Ryan was one of the hardest throwers in baseball history. He used his fastball to garner seven no-hitters and 324 wins over his 27-year career.

The New York Mets drafted Lynn Nolan Ryan (born 1947) in 1965. He reached the majors permanently in 1968 and was a key member of the 1969 "Miracle Mets," setting an NLCS record for most strikeouts by a reliever.

Ryan was traded to the Angels in 1971 for Jim Fregosi. In 1972, he was 19-16 with a league-leading 329 Ks. In 1973, he threw two no-hitters, set a single-season record with 383 strikeouts, and collected his first 20-win season. His

heater picked up the "Ryan Express" appellation in reference to the film *Von Ryan's Express*. During his eight seasons with California, he led the American League in strikeouts seven times (and in walks on six occasions).

In 1980, Ryan signed a free-agent deal with the Houston Astros to be close to his Texas home. Nolan thrived at the Astrodome, pacing the National League with a 1.69 ERA in 1981. He also led the loop in ERA and strikeouts in 1987, but finished just 8-16 due to poor support. In the 1980s, he improved his control significantly, going from a high of 204 walks in 1977 to totals under 100 over his last ten years. He signed

with Texas in 1989, and pitched for the Rangers for the remaining five seasons of his career.

Ryan, the only pitcher with three straight seasons of 300 or more strikeouts, is also the sole major-league hurler with more than four no-hitters. He tossed his fifth on national television in the heat of the 1981 pennant race. His seventh gem came in 1991 against the Toronto Blue Jays, when Ryan was 44 years old. He won eleven strikeout crowns, finished with a total of 5,174 Ks, and threw bullets until the day he retired in 1993.

Ryne Sandberg

Phillies president Bill Giles was so eager to trade Larry Bowa to the Cubs for Ivan DeJesus in 1981 that he threw in Ryne Sandberg, who went on to become baseball's best second baseman of the 1980s and the early '90s.

Ryne Dee Sandberg, born in 1959 in Spokane, Washington, starred in three sports in high school and was drafted by the Phillies in 1978.

In his Cub debut in 1982, Sandberg played 140 games at third base. He hit .271 and scored 103 runs. Moved to second base the last month of the season, he quickly adapted to his new position. In 1983, Sandberg became the first NL player to win a Gold Glove in his first season at a new position.

Sandberg led Chicago into their first NLCS appearance in 1984 by clubbing 19 home runs, batting .314, winning another Gold Glove, and leading the league with 114 runs and 19 triples. For his efforts, he was named the loop's Most Valuable Player.

The next year, Sandberg became the third player

SANDBERG HAS BEEN A FAN FAVORITE AT CHICAGO'S WRIGLEY FIELD.

ever with 25 home runs and 50 stolen bases in a season. Sandberg's 54 swipes were the most by a Cub since Frank Chance's 57 in 1906.

Sandberg broke a National League record in 1986 by making just five errors all season. In 1989, his 30 home runs led the Cubs to another NL East title. In 1990, Sandberg powered a loop-best 40 homers. Ryne was the first second sacker since Rogers Hornsby in 1925 to lead the league in homers.

Sandberg's surprise retirement in June 1994 brought to a close a tremendous, Hall-of-Fame caliber career. The friendly confines of Wrigley Field may never again see a second baseman with such a high degree of dedication and professionalism.

Ron Santo

Ron Santo may be best remembered as the leader of the ill-fated 1969 Cubs squad, but from 1960 to 1973, he was the top all-around third baseman in the National League.

The Cubs brought Ronald Edward Santo (born 1940) to the majors

SANTO FINISHED WITH A CAREER AVERAGE OF .277 WITH 1,331 RBI.

in 1960 after less than two full seasons of pro ball. In 1961, his first full big-league season, he batted .284 with 23 home runs and 83 RBI.

Santo came into his own in 1963, batting .297 with 25 homers and 99 RBI. In 1964 he hit 30 more dingers with 96 RBI and a career-best .313 average. Meanwhile, Santo drove in over 100 runs four times, including a high of 123 in 1969. A very patient hitter, Ron led the league four times in walks and hit over .300 three times. He was a nine-time All-Star.

Santo was a victim of the Cubs' youth movement after the 1973 season despite his 20 home runs. Chicago dealt him to the Angels, but Santo invoked the "five-and-ten" clause that allowed players with ten years experience, and

five on one club, to deny a trade. He wanted to stay in Chicago, so he was instead sent to the White Sox. However, the Sox used Santo at second base, then first base, and finally at designated hitter in 1974. The switching hindered Santo, who hit just .221 before retiring after his south side season with 2,254 career hits.

Santo was also the best defensive third baseman in the NL during the 1960s, and he won Gold Gloves every year from 1964 to 1968.

Unbeknownst to most fans during his playing career, Santo suffers from diabetes. He remains a spokesman in the fight against the disease today and serves as a radio announcer for his beloved Cubs.

Mike Schmidt

Young Mike Schmidt was Philadelphia's starting third baseman in 1973. He hit 18 homers but batted a paltry .196 and fanned 136 times in only 367 at bats. From that beginning, Schmidt went on to become one of the best third basemen in baseball history.

Michael Jack Schmidt (born 1949) was a college All-American at Ohio University and was drafted by the Phillies in 1971. Schmidt prospered in Eugene in 1972, posting a .291 average with 26 home runs and 91 RBI.

After his dismal 1973 season, Schmidt could have easily lost his job, but the Phillies' faith in him paid off the next year. He won his first of eight National League home run crowns with 36 blasts, drove in 116 runs, and pumped his average to .282. He also won homer crowns in 1975 and '76 with 38 dingers each year. Schmidt was a twelve-time All-Star, and helped the Phillies win six NLCS titles.

Schmidt's best season came in 1980, when his league-leading 48 dingers and 121 RBI led the

SCHMIDT HIT MORE HOME RUNS THAN ANY THIRD BASEMAN IN BASEBALL.

Phillies to their first World Championship. In the Series, he batted .381 with three homers and seven RBI. Mike was named both the NL Most Valuable Player and the World Series MVP that year.

Only Hank Aaron and Willie Mays hit more National League round-trippers than Schmidt's 542. He topped 30 homers 13 times, and surpassed the 35-homer barrier 11 times. Only Babe Ruth's nine league home run titles top Schmidt's eight crowns.

Schmidt was the best defensive third baseman in the league for several seasons, winning ten Gold Gloves. He also broke numerous NL fielding records. He retired in 1989 after playing his entire career with the Phillies.

Tom Seaver

Tom Seaver's 25 wins carried the New York Mets to a stunning pennant in 1969 and earned him the nickname "Tom Terrific." In his 20-year career, Seaver set a multitude of Met and National League pitching records.

Unlike most pitching greats, George Thomas Seaver (born 1944) did not attract the notice of major league scouts until he was in college. The Braves offered him a $40,000 bonus in 1966 to sign. The contract was voided, however, by commissioner William Eckert, who held a lottery for any team who agreed to match or top the Braves' offer. The Mets stepped in, picked the lucky number, and signed Seaver.

In 1969, 1973, and 1975, he won Cy Young Awards, and twice hurled the Mets to a pennant. The team's second flag came in 1973 when Seaver won 19 games and paced the NL in ERA and strikeouts. In all, Seaver paced the senior circuit five times in whiffs and fanned over 200 men a season a record nine straight seasons. His 3,640 punchouts are fourth on the all-time list.

In 1977, Seaver was traded to Cincinnati. After six years in Cincinnati, the Mets reacquired him before the 1983 season. After a 9-14 campaign, however, he was drafted by the Chicago White Sox.

Seaver won 31 games in his first two seasons in Chicago, and nailed down his 300th career victory in 1985. When he began poorly in 1986, he was dealt to Boston. He retired after the

WITH THE REDS, SEAVER TWICE LED THE NL IN WINNING PERCENTAGE.

season with a .603 career winning percentage, the highest of any 300-game winner in the past half-century. Seaver was overwhelmingly named to the Hall of Fame in 1992.

Al Simmons

Al Simmons's career .334 average mocked those who criticized his peculiar penchant for striding toward third base when he swung. The unorthodox batting style led to the tag "Bucketfoot Al," but Simmons had the last laugh when he reached the Hall of Fame.

Aloys Szymanski (1902-1956) never wanted to be anything but a baseball player. In 1922, he signed his first contract with the Milwaukee Brewers of the American Association. When Al hit .398 in 24 games in 1923, the Philadelphia Athletics bought him for around $50,000.

In 1924, his rookie year, Simmons batted .308 and knocked home 102 runs. The following year, he collected a league-leading 253 hits, hiked his average to .387, and became the first player in American League history to drive in 100 or more runs in each of his first two seasons in the majors.

Simmons hit 307 lifetime home runs and was also a good outfielder with a strong arm. When Ty Cobb joined the A's in 1927, he helped Al to develop even further. Simmons, in fact, found it easy to befriend the much-shunned Cobb. In his dedication to becoming the best player possible, Simmons himself acquired a reputation for not being overly personable.

The A's took three straight pennants starting in 1929, and Al enjoyed the first of five straight seasons of 200 or more hits. The following year he won his first of two consecutive batting crowns and was generally regarded as the AL's best player.

Simmons was traded to the Chicago White Sox in 1933 for economic reasons. Later Al played for Detroit, Washington, and Boston before spending one season in the NL He returned to the A's in 1944 to finish his career. A coach for the A's during the 1940s, Simmons acted as unofficial manager when Connie Mack grew too old to serve capably.

George Sisler

George Sisler was one of the best first basemen who ever played the game. Injuries allowed him to play at peak capacity for only half of his career. With luck, however, he might have been the greatest hitter of them all.

George Harold Sisler (1893-1973) of Akron, Ohio, signed a pro contract while still in high school. He later enrolled at the University of Michigan to play under Branch Rickey. His contract was bought by Pittsburgh, but George also signed with Rickey's St. Louis Browns. The National Commission ruled in favor of the Browns.

Sisler began his career as a pitcher. After joining the Browns, in fact, he outdueled Walter Johnson. Playing first base in 1916,

Sisler hit .305 in his first full season. After three successive years of batting around .350, George went wild in 1920. Not only did he top the American League with a .407 average, but he collected an all-time record 257 hits and clouted 19 home runs. Sisler almost never struck out, led the AL four times in stolen bases, and played fine defense.

In 1922, Sisler raised the ante by batting .420. He also paced the AL in runs, steals, hits, and triples, and won the league's MVP Award. Even with all Sisler's heroics, the Browns still finished second to the Yankees by a single game.

Unfortunately, George began to develop double

vision, stemming from his infected sinuses. He missed all of 1923, and an operation only partially remedied the problem. When Sisler returned in 1924, he slumped to .305. He never

GEORGE SISLER LED HIS LEAGUE IN FIELDING PERCENTAGE EIGHT TIMES.

felt he was quite the same player and closed his major-league career with the Senators and the Boston Braves.

Sisler ended his career in 1928. Father of three sons who played pro ball, he joined the Hall of Fame in 1939.

Ozzie Smith

Just like the mythical Wizard of Oz, Ozzie Smith made everything look easy. He fielded almost flawlessly at shortstop, hit better than most shortstops, and stole bases with ease.

Osborne Earl Smith (born 1954) did not sign a pro contract until age 22 because he wanted to finish college. The San Diego Padres drafted him in 1977.

Smith started 1978 as San Diego's shortstop, notching 40 stolen bases and pacing the league with 28 sacrifice hits. For his efforts, he finished second in Rookie of the Year balloting. He also registered 548 assists, the first of a record eight times he tallied 500 or more assists.

A defining play in Smith's career came that April. Ozzie dove to his left for a Jeff Burroughs roller and, as the ball unexpectedly bounced up, he amazingly grabbed it bare-handed and threw Burroughs out. In 1979, Smith led the National League shortstops with 555 assists, and won his first of an amazing 13 straight Gold Gloves the next year. Smith also stole 57 bases in 1980.

On February 11, 1982, Smith was traded to the Cardinals for star shortstop Garry Templeton. Some felt the Padres won the trade, but the reverse turned out to be true. Smith became an even more valuable defender in Busch Stadium than he had been in San Diego, and he chipped in offensively. The Cards won the World Series the year Ozzie joined the team.

He developed line-drive power, began drawing more walks, and hit .270 or over almost every year. In 1985, he hit .276 with six homers. His home run won game five of the NLCS. Smith's best season was 1987, when his .303 average, 182 hits, 104 runs scored, and 75 RBI led to a second-place MVP finish. Ozzie really did get better with age, and has carved out a position for himself among the all-time great shortstops.

Duke Snider

An unprecedented concentration of talent played center field in New York in the 1950s. The Yankees had Mickey Mantle, the Giants had Willie Mays, and Duke Snider played for Brooklyn. From 1954 to 1957, Snider had the most home runs and RBI of the three, and he totaled more homers and RBI than any player of the 1950s.

Born in 1926 in Compton, California, Edwin Donald Snider signed with the Dodgers in 1944. He played his first game for the Dodgers the same day that Jackie Robinson did, in 1947. However, Snider, a good minor-league hitter, hit just .241 with 24 strikeouts in 83 at bats before being demoted to St. Paul. Snider

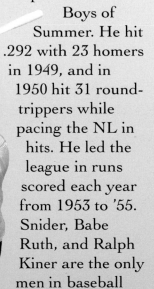

spent most of 1948 in Montreal, where Branch Rickey put Duke through a strict regimen to teach him the strike zone. Snider learned enough to walk 80 or more times four straight seasons.

Soon, Snider delivered lefthanded power for the Boys of Summer. He hit .292 with 23 homers in 1949, and in 1950 hit 31 round-trippers while pacing the NL in hits. He led the league in runs scored each year from 1953 to '55. Snider, Babe Ruth, and Ralph Kiner are the only men in baseball

history to hit at least 40 homers five straight times.

The Duke, a regular on six Dodger pennant winners, hit four homers twice in World Series competition and ranks fourth with 11 home runs in Series play. Snider also totaled an impressive .594 slugging percentage in World Series competition. In addition to belting 407 lifetime home runs, Snider also played outstanding defense and had a great throwing arm.

Knee and elbow injuries reduced Duke to part-time play beginning in 1960. He spent a year with the Mets in 1963, enjoying his familiar New York (but not the Mets), and retired after a year with the Giants in 1964. A broadcaster for the Expos in the 1970s, Snider joined the Hall of Fame in 1980.

Warren Spahn

Warren Spahn's 363 wins are still more than any other left-hander in history. Despite not winning his first big-league game until age 25, he anchored Braves' staffs for almost twenty years. Spahn led the NL in wins a record eight times, complete games a record nine times, and strikeouts four years in a row.

Born in Buffalo in 1921, Warren Edward Spahn was the son of an avid amateur baseball player. Warren grew up as a first baseman, but soon switched to pitching. Signed by the Braves in 1940, he led the Three-I League in 1941 with 19 wins and a 1.83 ERA. Spahn was off to

war for the next three years, where he earned a Bronze Star and a Purple Heart.

Warren returned in 1946 and went 8-5. He bloomed in 1947, winning 21 and leading the NL with a 2.33 ERA. In 1948, he teamed with Johnny Sain in the famous "Spahn and Sain and pray for rain" rotation. Sain won 24, Warren took 15, and the Braves won the pennant.

In 1949, Spahn led the NL in victories, complete games, innings, and strikeouts. He paced the loop with 21 wins and 191 Ks in 1950. Spahn then captured 22 in 1951, a league-best 23 in 1953, 21 in 1954, and 20 in

1956. After losing velocity on his fastball, he simply developed new pitches and depended on his vast knowledge of NL hitters.

SPAHN WITH ROTATION-MATE JOHNNY SAIN—A FORMIDABLE DUO.

Spahn went 21-11 in 1957 and 22-11 in 1958 as the Braves captured two pennants and a World Series. The seemingly ageless hurler cleared 20 wins from 1959 to '61 and again in 1963 before retiring in 1965. Warren still ranks in the top ten of career wins, innings pitched, and shutouts.

Tris Speaker

The evidence shows that Tris Speaker was the best center fielder of his era, if not ever. He revolutionized outfield play more than any other player in history. In addition, Speaker was also a tremendous batsman who collected 3,514 career hits.

Born in Hubbard, Texas, Tristram E. Speaker (1888-1958) started in baseball as a pitcher. When converted to the outfield, Speaker played such a shallow center field that he was, in effect, a fifth infielder. In the dead-ball era, when long drives were rare, other outfielders copied Speaker to cut down on bloop hits. In the lively ball era of the early 1920s, Speaker was the only center fielder who could continue to play shallow and still chase down long hits. He possessed great speed, unparalleled instincts, and a strong throwing arm.

Tris joined the Red Sox in 1908. In 1912, Speaker played on his first of two World Championship teams in the Hub while pacing the American League in doubles, home runs, and on-base percentage. During his career, "The Grey Eagle" topped the junior circuit in two-base hits a record eight times. His 792 doubles are still more than any other player in history. He batted over .300 18 times, and his .345 average is fifth on the all-time list.

A salary dispute resulted in a trade to Cleveland after the 1915 season. In 1916, Tris hit .386 to win the batting crown. In July 1919, the Indians named Speaker player-manager. The next year, Cleveland gained its first pennant as Tris batted .388.

In 1926, when implicated in a game-fixing scandal involving Ty Cobb, Speaker quit the Indians. He and Cobb were exonerated, though, when their accuser, former pitcher Dutch Leonard, refused to confront the pair in person. Speaker returned to play two more seasons, and was enshrined in the Hall of Fame in 1937.

Willie Stargell

Willie Stargell was a mainstay of the Pittsburgh Pirates for 21 years. He retired among the all-time leaders in home runs, slugging, and RBI, and was elected to the Hall of Fame in 1988.

Wilver Dornel Stargell (born 1940) of Alameda, California, was signed by the Pirates in 1959. In 1962, Stargell hit 27 home runs in the International League, and was called up to Pittsburgh for good.

Stargell took over left field for the Bucs in '63 and hit .243 with 11 homers. Playing half his games in Forbes Field hurt his power stats, but he started a string of 13 straight 20-homer seasons in 1964. He retired in 1982 with a .282 career average and 475 round-trippers, and is the only man to hit two balls clear out of Dodger Stadium.

Only in the seventies, after the Pirates moved to Three Rivers Stadium, did Willie get his due. In 1971 the Pirates won the NL pennant, and Willie led the league with 48 homers. He scored 104 runs and knocked in 125. The Bucs won six NL East titles during the 1970s, and Stargell's 269 homers were the highest total of the decade. Injuries forced a move to first base, and from 1974 to '77, his home run totals declined. In 1978, however, "Pops" came back to bat .295 with 28 homers and 97 RBI.

In 1979, Stargell led the Bucs to the World Championship. Though he played in just 126 games, he hit .281 with 32 home runs, and then batted over .400 with five homers in the playoffs and Series. He tied with Keith Hernandez in the voting for the NL MVP

IN 1973 WILLIE STARGELL LED THE NATIONAL LEAGUE WITH 44 HOMERS.

Award, and captured the NLCS and World Series MVPs. Honored both for his leadership and his production, he encouraged the Pirates' "Fam-i-lee" by example and in spirit.

Sam Thompson

Samuel Luther Thompson (1860-1922) was a 24-year-old carpenter in his hometown of Danville, Indiana, when a scout for the Evansville club in the Northwest League bade him to give professional baseball a try. Thompson agreed, believing that the $2.50 per game deal was equitable, and ended up in the Hall of Fame.

Joining the NL's Detroit Wolverines in July 1885, Thompson tallied 11 hits in his first 26 at bats and claimed the club's right field job. He led Detroit in batting in 1886, his first full campaign in the majors. In 1887, he paced the entire NL, hitting .372, and bagged a 19th-century record 166 RBI. Still, Thompson's talents went largely unrecognized in his time (RBI totals were not an official statistic). As a result, it was only after Thompson retired that historians revealed him to be the most prolific of any player ever at driving in runs—.921 per game. The home run, another Thompson specialty, was regarded as a trivial accomplishment in the late 1800s, but his lifetime total of 127 home runs is the second-highest tally of the 1876-1892 era.

Thompson, however, was not merely a slugger. He also led the National League on three occasions in hits, twice in doubles, and once in triples. A good outfielder, he had one of the strongest arms in the game.

The Detroit Wolverine franchise collapsed after the 1888 season, and Sam was sold to the Phillies.

In the early 1890s, Big Sam was joined by Ed Delahanty and Billy Hamilton, giving Philadelphia a trio of future Hall-of-Fame outfielders. While Hamilton batted .399, the other two topped the .400 mark in 1894. The following year, Thompson hit .392 and led the National League with 18 homers and 165 RBI. A bad back shelved him early in 1897, and despite several comeback attempts, his career was for all intents and purposes finished. In 1906, at age 46, he appeared in eight games with Detroit, playing in the outfield with a 19-year-old rookie named Ty Cobb.

Arky Vaughan

A nine-time All-Star, Arky Vaughan was one of the greatest offensive shortstops in baseball history, second only to the magnificent Honus Wagner. He led the NL three times in walks, triples, runs scored, and on-base percentage. Vaughan also paced the league in putouts and assists thrice.

Born in Clifton, Arkansas, Joseph Floyd Vaughan (1912-1952) was raised in Fullerton, California. After playing semipro ball, he was signed in 1931 by Wichita of the Western Association, where he hit .338 with 21 homers and 145 runs scored. The Pirates made Arky their starting shortstop in 1932.

In 1935, he hit .385 to lead the National League, slugged 19 home runs, and drove in 99. An outstanding contact hitter, he walked 118 times in 1936 while fanning just 21. He never totaled more than 38 strikeouts in a season. In the 1941 All-Star game, Vaughan became the first player to hit two home runs in a midsummer classic. That season, he led the NL in runs scored and triples while batting .300.

After ten seasons in Pittsburgh, Vaughan was dealt to the Dodgers, as the Pirates attempted to rebuild the franchise with youth. In 1943, he led the National League in runs scored and stolen bases. However, the mild-mannered Vaughan could not abide Brooklyn manager Leo Durocher. When the Dodgers would not trade him, Vaughan retired at age 31. He missed the next three seasons, returning only in 1947 when Durocher was suspended for the year. He hit .325 off the bench and saw action in his first World Series. The Yankees, however, bested the Dodgers in seven. After slumping to .244 in 1948, he retired for good. Had he not missed those prime years, Vaughan might have approached 3,000 career hits. Vaughan retired with a .318 career average, the second highest ever by a shortstop.

In 1952, Vaughan drowned in a fishing mishap near Eagleville, California. The Hall of Fame Veterans Committee passed over Vaughan several times before he was selected in 1985.

Honus Wagner

John Peter Wagner (1874-1955) was a rarity, the son of an immigrant father who thought baseball was an acceptable profession. By 1898, Honus was an established hitting star with Louisville of the National League, although he did not have a regular defensive spot. The Colonels used him at several positions. When the franchise folded in 1899, owner Barney Dreyfuss, who also owned the Pittsburgh Pirates, took Wagner and several other Colonels stars with him to Pittsburgh.

Wagner played 135 games, mostly in the outfield, for the Bucs in 1900, won the first of his record eight NL batting titles, and also led the loop in doubles, triples, and slugging average. Wagner played half the 1901 season at shortstop, but returned to the outfield in 1902, hit .330, and led the NL in runs, doubles, and RBI. The Pirates won the pennant by a record 27½ games, and then survived several defections to the American League to win a third successive crown in 1903. Player-manager Fred Clarke gave Honus the shortstop job permanently that season, and "The Flying Dutchman" became a defensive force at the position.

Wagner, a speedy, strong, and graceful player, dominated the NL in the early 1900s. He won four straight batting titles between 1906 and '09, won five stolen base crowns, and paced the loop seven times in doubles. During his 21-year career, Wagner led the league at least twice in every major offensive department except home runs and walks.

When he retired in 1917 as a living legend, he had compiled 3,571 hits, and more runs, total bases, RBI, and stolen bases than any other player to that point. These records have since been broken, but no other shortstop in the game has neared Wagner's achievements. Honus was a beloved player and public figure, and was one of the first five players named to the Hall of Fame in 1936.

Ed Walsh

Originally, Hall-of-Famer Edward Augustine Walsh (1881-1959) had an overpowering fastball and little else. In 1904, however, he learned the spitball from White Sox teammate Elmer Stricklett, reputedly the first to master the pitch. Of Walsh's spitter, Sam Crawford once said, "I think the ball disintegrated on the way to the plate and the catcher put it back together again."

Walsh led the AL with ten shutouts in 1906, and in 1907 won 24 games, worked 422 innings, and collected a pitchers' all-time record 227 assists. The following year, Big Ed labored an American League record 464 innings, hurled 42 complete games, and became the last big-league pitcher to notch 40 victories in a season. Unfortunately, the weak-hitting White Sox still finished third. That October 2, Walsh ceded Cleveland just one run and fanned 15 batters but lost 1-0 when Addie Joss threw a perfect game.

That game was typical of Walsh's fate during his 13 years with the White Sox. Two years later, when he led the AL with a magnificent 1.26 ERA, he nonetheless had a losing record (18-20) as the Sox hit just .211 for the season.

Despite little offensive support, Walsh never lacked for confidence. Charles Dryden called him the only man who "could strut while standing still." Ring Lardner made Big Ed his model for Jack Keefe, the cocky hero of *You Know Me, Al: A Busher's Letters,* the classic work of baseball fiction of the era.

Playing for the penurious Charlie Comiskey, Walsh was forced to work many

HARD-WORKING ED WALSH LED THE AL FOUR TIMES IN INNINGS PITCHED.

innings for meager pay. By 1913, this overwork had taken its toll, and he won only 13 games in his last five seasons. He ended his career with "just" 195 wins, but more than compensated with a 1.82 career ERA—the lowest of all time.

Paul Waner

Paul Glee Waner (1903-1965) left East Central Teachers College in Oklahoma against his father's advice to pursue a professional baseball career in 1923. Signed by Dick Williams of the San Francisco Seals, Waner never looked back. Originally a pitcher, he switched to the outfield after suffering an arm injury in the Pacific Coast League. With the Seals in 1925, Waner paced the PCL with a .401 batting average and 75 doubles.

Sold to Pittsburgh that winter, Paul immediately began to demonstrate that he was cheap even at the high price the Bucs paid for him. In 1926, his rookie season, he hit .336, second best in the National League. "Big Poison" Paul's performance spurred the Pirates to buy his younger brother Lloyd, who became "Little Poison." The two combined to amass a sibling record 460 hits and bring the Pirates a National League pennant in 1927. That year, Paul led the NL with a .380 average, 237 hits, 17 triples, and 131 RBI to win the MVP Award.

Paul developed into one of the finest hitters in National League history. He won three hitting titles and led the NL at one time or another in every major batting department except home runs and walks. En route to accumulating 3,152 career hits, he set an NL record by tabulating 200 or more hits in a season eight separate times. His 191 triples are the tenth-best total of all time, and in 1932, Paul hit 62 doubles. Waner usually walked 70 times in a season, and finished his career with a .333 average. He was an outstanding flycatcher, combining a center fielder's speed with one of the strongest arms in the league.

Waner closed out his career with Brooklyn and the Boston Braves and was named to the Hall of Fame in 1952. He returned to the game in 1957 as a batting instructor with the Milwaukee Braves. Later he served in a similar capacity with the Cardinals and the Phillies. A great hitter who could also teach hitting skills, Waner wrote a well-received book on the subject in the early 1960s.

Hoyt Wilhelm

Hoyt Wilhelm blazed the trail for the modern relief specialist, and was the first career reliever to enter the Hall of Fame. He entered more games than any pitcher ever, and retired with more relief wins than anyone else.

James Hoyt Wilhelm (born 1923) grew up in North Carolina as a fan of Washington Senators' pitcher Dutch Leonard, one of the first hurlers to rely almost exclusively on the knuckleball. Eventually, Wilhelm himself became a master of the elusive pitch.

A winner of the Purple Heart in World War II, Wilhelm was a starting pitcher in the minors. He spent eight seasons in the bushes, lost three more years to the war, and did not make his big-league debut until he was 28.

In 1952, Hoyt made the Giants as a reliever, bursting out of nowhere to lead the National League with 71 games pitched, 15 relief wins, and a 2.43 ERA. He led the league in appearances in 1953, and notched 15 saves. In 1954, Wilhelm posted a 2.10 ERA and a league-best 12 relief wins as the Giants won the World Series.

Soon, however, he lost favor with the Giants. The Orioles converted him back to the starting rotation in 1958. Wilhelm promptly tossed a no-hitter that year and then led the AL in 1959 with a 2.19 ERA. Ultimately, he ended up back in the bullpen.

From 1962 to '68, with the Orioles and the White Sox, he registered ERAs below 2.00 six of the seven years. The ageless Wilhelm rolled on, pitching effectively through the early 1970s, and finished his career at age 49 with the 1972 Dodgers. He totaled 227 career saves, including a personal best 27 in 1964 with the White Sox.

Like those of other baseball pioneers, many of Wilhelm's career totals have been eclipsed. His total of 1,070 career games still stands. Even if that mark, too, is broken, Wilhelm's place in history— and in the Hall of Fame—is secure.

Ted Williams

Ted Williams's dream was to have people point to him and say "There goes the greatest hitter who ever lived." Many baseball historians make that claim.

Born in 1918 in San Diego, Theodore Samuel Williams was inked by the Red Sox in 1938. The brash youngster won the American Association Triple Crown with a .366 average, 43 homers, and 142 RBI.

In 1939, Williams made an immediate impact in Boston, hitting .327 with 31 home runs and a league-leading 145 RBI. In 1941 he hit .406; nobody has cleared .400 since. In 1942, Williams produced his first Triple Crown, with a .356 average, 36 home runs, and 137 RBI, only to finish second in MVP voting.

WILLIAMS PERFECTED THE ART AND SCIENCE OF HITTING A BASEBALL.

Williams lost three years to World War II serving as a pilot with the Marines, but returned in 1946 to win his first MVP Award. Ted captured his second Triple Crown in 1947 but was again denied the MVP. The "Splendid Splinter" won the batting crown in 1948 and another MVP in 1949, hitting .343 with a league-leading 43 homers, 159 RBI, 150 runs, and 162 walks.

Ted spent most of 1952-53 fighting in Korea. He again won batting crowns in 1957and 1958. Williams retired after the 1960 campaign, homering in his last big-league at bat.

His .483 on-base average is the highest ever, and in five seasons he reached base over half the time. Ted also owns the second-best slugging average and 521 home runs. He did all this despite missing five seasons to war. "Teddy Ballgame" was inducted into Cooperstown in 1966 and managed the Washington Senators from 1969 to '74.

Dave Winfield

Born in St. Paul, Minnesota, in 1951, David Mark Winfield was an amazing athlete by the time of his high school graduation. He was drafted by the Orioles, but chose to attend the University of Minnesota, where he played baseball and basketball. In 1973, Winfield was the Padres' first-round draft pick. In addition, he was also drafted by football's Minnesota Vikings, the NBA's Atlanta Hawks, and the ABA's New Orleans Jazz.

Winfield signed with the Padres, skipping the minors entirely and landing in the Padres' outfield. He batted .277 with three homers in 56 games. Full-time outfield work followed in 1974, and although he led the league with 12 errors, Winfield also slugged 20 homers and collected 75 RBI.

Dave broke loose with 25 homers and 92 RBI in 1977. He hit .300 each of the next two years, with 58 total homers and 215 total RBI. His fielding improved, and he earned his first of seven Gold Gloves in 1979. Winfield also showed a tremendous throwing arm.

After the 1980 season, Winfield elected free agency and signed with the Yankees. He became baseball's highest-paid player at that time. In New York, he was successful on the field and controversial out of uniform. Winfield's 1988 autobiography offered unbridled criticism of Yankee owner George Steinbrenner, who himself called Winfield "Mr. May," in reference to Dave's supposed inability to hit like "Mr. October," Reggie Jackson, in the clutch.

A twelve-time All-Star, Winfield hit 37 dingers in 1982 and 32 in 1983. Between 1982 and '89, his lowest RBI total was 97. He sat out the 1989 season with a herniated disk, but returned at age 38 in 1990 to hit 21 homers and win the Comeback Player of the Year Award. In 1992, he collected 108 RBI and helped the Blue Jays win the World Championship.

In 1993, Winfield was signed by his hometown Twins. That September Winfield responded by collecting his 3,000th career hit.

Carl Yastrzemski

A great hitter for several seasons and a very good hitter for many more, Carl Yastrzemski performed the impossible—replacing Ted Williams—well enough to make the Hall of Fame.

Carl Michael Yastrzemski (born 1939) of Southampton, New York, was pursued by several pro teams, but spurned them to attend Notre Dame in 1958. After one year, he turned professional and signed with the Red Sox. In 1959, he led the Carolina League with a .377 batting average, and in 1960 paced the American Association with 193 hits.

Williams retired after 1960, and Yaz took his left field spot. He batted .266 in his first season and improved to .296 with 94 RBI in 1962. Carl won his first batting title in 1963 at .321, and showed power and patience. He ultimately walked over 100 times in six seasons.

In 1965, he led the AL with a .536 slugging percentage and 45 doubles, and in 1966 led the circuit with 39 doubles.

The Red Sox, a ninth-place team in 1966, won the pennant on the last day of a wild 1967 season. Yaz, hitting .326 with a career-best 44 homers, became the last man to win a Triple Crown by hitting .522 in the final two weeks of the season and was named the AL MVP. In the World Series, he hit .400, but the Sox lost in seven.

In 1968, Carl won another batting title, and hit 40 homers in both 1969 and 1970. Ted Williams said that Yaz "reminded me of myself at that age...he positively quivered waiting for that next pitch." Yaz swung

GRITTY AND DURABLE, YAZ DELIGHTED BOSTON FANS FOR 23 SEASONS.

a big bat for 23 seasons and patrolled left field expertly for the Red Sox.

Yastrzemski collected his 3,000th hit in 1979 and retired in 1983 with 452 homers and a .285 average. Cooperstown called his name in 1989.

Cy Young

Upon being signed by Canton of the Tri-State League in 1890, the 23-year-old Young was seen warming up against a wooden fence. The ensuing damage to the barrier was likened to that of a cyclone hitting a wall. A sportswriter shortened "cyclone" to "Cy."

Denton True Young (1867-1955) joined the Cleveland Spiders later that year. Cap Anson, player-manager of the Chicago White Stockings, rejected Young earlier that year as being "just another big farmer." After Cy beat Chicago in his first major-league outing, Anson tried in vain to purchase him.

Throughout the 1890s, Young was the top pitcher in the game, blending stamina, guile, and excellent control. However, when attendance sagged in Cleveland, Young and most of the team's other stars were shipped to St. Louis in 1899.

YOUNG PITCHED FOR TWO PENNANT-WINNING BOSTON AMERICANS CLUBS.

Turning 33 in 1900, Young registered just 19 wins, his lowest output since his rookie season. Cy then signed with Boston in the new American League. Rumors of Young's decline were dispelled as he led the yearling major league in wins in 1901, then repeated his feat the next two years.

Cy won 20 or more games six times for the Boston Americans and participated in the first modern World Series in 1903. Perhaps the finest effort of his career came on May 5, 1904, when he pitched a perfect game against Rube Waddell and the Philadelphia Athletics.

Young retired in 1911 with 511 career victories, 7,357 innings pitched, and no sore arm. Cy was inducted into the Hall of Fame in 1938. Shortly after Young's death, Commissioner Ford Frick originated the Cy Young Award, an annual honor bestowed upon the pitcher deemed most valuable in each league.